THE
STRONG
FAMILY

From the Bible-teaching ministry of

Charles R. Swindoll

INSIGHT FOR LIVING

Chuck graduated in 1963 from Dallas Theological Seminary, where he now serves as the school's fourth president, helping to prepare a new generation of men and women for the ministry. Chuck has served in pastorates in three states: Massachusetts, Texas, and California, including almost twenty-three years at the First Evangelical Free Church in Fullerton, California. His sermon messages have been aired over radio since 1979 as the *Insight for Living* broadcast. A best-selling author, Chuck has written numerous books and booklets on many subjects.

Based on the outlines and transcripts of Chuck's sermons, the study guide text is authored by Ken Gire, a graduate of Texas Christian University and Dallas Theological Seminary. The Living Insights are written by Lee Hough, a graduate of The University of Texas at Arlington and Dallas Theological Seminary.

Editor in Chief:
Cynthia Swindoll

Coauthor of Text:
Ken Gire

Author of Living Insights:
Lee Hough

Assistant Editor, First and Revised Editions:
Wendy Peterson

Copy Editors:
Brown Suffield
Marco Salazar

Graphics System Administrator:
Bob Haskins

Director, Communications Division:
Carla Meberg

Project Manager:
Alene Cooper

Project Coordinators:
Susan Nelson
Colette Muse

Print Production Manager:
Deedee Snyder

Assistant Production Manager:
John Norton

Unless otherwise identified, all Scripture references are from the New American Standard Bible, © The Lockman Foundation 1960, 1962, 1963, 1968, 1971, 1972, 1973, 1975, 1977. Used by permission. Other translations cited are *The Revised English Bible* [REB] and *The Living Bible* [LB].

ISBN 1-57972-008-0
COVER PHOTOGRAPH: Superstock
COVER DESIGN: Mark Veldheer
Printed in the United States of America

CONTENTS

Editor's Note

When Chuck wrote *Growing Wise in Family Life* in 1988, we developed a cassette album series and study guide by the same name but with differing sermon and lesson titles. In revising the book and renaming it *The Strong Family,* we decided to take advantage of the opportunity to revise the sermon titles from which Chuck had developed the chapters in the book, thus making it easier for individuals and Bible study groups to correlate all the material.

It will also be noted that our cassette series and guide have three messages not used in developing any chapters in the book. These sermons have been added to provide further poignant illustrations and amplifications of the material. "A Chip off the Old Bent" correlates with the two messages "Your Baby Has the Bents." "When Brothers and Sisters Battle" and "Releasing the Reins" are messages that fit very appropriately with the section titled "Weathering the Storms."

INTRODUCTION

Everything I read these days assures me that the family is "in." Many of the books, television shows, and movies now in the marketplace are centering attention on domestic scenes. Clearly, the "hot ticket" is family life.

But wait. Even though all this is true, who says that what is being portrayed on page and stage is accurate? The more we see of what is being produced by the secular media, the more we realize how unbiblical (and often how unwholesome) the material is. What good is it if the family is "in" but God's timeless wisdom is "out"? Seems to me that our need today is for fresh and forthright insight from our ever-relevant Lord, whose Word is still unsurpassed when it comes to reliable information.

That, in a nutshell, explains why I have chosen to prepare and present this study, which places proper emphasis on wisdom in family living. If my words of instruction bring you back to the principles of Scripture, causing you to discover biblical truth and how to put it into action, my goal will have been reached . . . my prayers will have been answered.

Chuck Swindoll

PUTTING TRUTH
INTO ACTION

K nowledge apart from application falls short of God's desire for His children. He wants us to apply what we learn so that we will change and grow. This study guide was prepared with these goals in mind. As you go through the following pages, we hope your desire to discover biblical truth will grow as your understanding of God's Word increases and that you will be encouraged to apply what you've learned.

To assist you in your study, we've included a section called Living Insights at the end of each lesson. These exercises will challenge you to study further and to think of specific ways to put your discoveries into action.

On occasion a lesson is followed by a Digging Deeper section, which gives you additional information and resources to probe further into some issues raised in that lesson.

There are many ways to use this guide—in personal devotions, group studies, discussions with friends and family, and Sunday school classes. And, of course, it's an ideal study aid when you're listening to its corresponding *Insight for Living* radio series.

To benefit most from this study guide, we would encourage you to consider it a spiritual journal. That's why we've included space in the Living Insights for recording your thoughts and discoveries. We hope you'll return to those sections often for review and encouragement as you continue to grow in your walk with Christ.

Ken Gire
Coauthor of Text

Lee Hough
Author of Living Insights

THE STRONG FAMILY

Chapter 1

AN ENDANGERED SPECIES?

Deuteronomy 6:1–24

The author who gave us *Future Shock*, Alvin Toffler, later wrote a book titled *The Third Wave*. In it he looks ahead to the year 2000 and beyond. He contends that the first wave which rolled over the earth was an agricultural one. The second was the wave of industry. The third, which is now upon us, is the wave of technology. About this third wave he writes:

> A powerful tide is surging across much of the world today, creating a new, often bizarre, environment in which to work, play, marry, raise children, or retire. In this bewildering context, businessmen swim against highly erratic economic currents; politicians see their ratings bob wildly up and down; universities, hospitals, and other institutions battle desperately against inflation. Value systems splinter and crash, while the lifeboats of family, church, and state are hurled madly about.[1]

According to Toffler, most people make the serious mistake of thinking and believing that the world they have known will extend and endure forever. But that isn't true. The third wave, which Toffler maintains we are now engaged in, makes a quantum leap from what we have known in the familiar waters of yesterday to the uncharted seas of tomorrow.

So we'll be swimming against the tide if we try to raise our families exactly as we were raised. The world is different today. And the challenge of keeping the genuinely Christian family from becoming an

---

1. Alvin Toffler, *The Third Wave* (London, England: Pan Books, 1980), p. 15.

endangered species is perhaps more difficult now than it has ever been.

That's the bad news. The good news is that the biblical principles for raising a family haven't changed. God's Word is still as watertight and able to save today as it was in Noah's day. But there is one requirement on our part—authenticity. Families attempting to circumnavigate this turbulent world on rafts made of thin religious veneers will splinter and sink. Only those whose faith is genuine, permeating the home, will survive. So, if we're going to meet the challenge before us—that of building genuinely Christian families—we must look to the essentials of authenticity.

Looking Within: The Essentials of Authenticity

As the Israelites prepared to enter the Promised Land, they, too, faced an intimidating challenge—to penetrate a pagan culture. It was a new wave Israel was moving into. The first had been slavery in Egypt. The second was the wave of wilderness wanderings. Now they were about to move into a third wave unlike anything they had known before. To prepare them for that challenge, Moses took them aside, reiterating the essentials of authentic faith that would help their families not only survive but succeed (compare Deut. 6:24 with 6:2).[2]

Regarding the Lord Our God

For Israel to survive successfully in the land, *parents had to be permeated by a love for God.*

> "Now this is the commandment, the statutes and
> the judgments which the Lord your God has com-
> manded me to teach you, that you might do them
> in the land where you are going over to possess it,
> so that you and your son and your grandson might fear
> the Lord your God, to keep all His statutes and His
> commandments, which I command you, all the days
> of your life, and that your days may be prolonged.
> O Israel, you should listen and be careful to do it,

---

2. Deuteronomy, Moses' last words to the nation before they entered Canaan, literally means "second law" (from *deutero*, meaning "second" and *nomos*, meaning "law"). Essentially, the book is a repetition of previously revealed instructions, serving to underscore their importance. This, by the way, is why the Ten Commandments are listed twice, once in Exodus 20 and again in Deuteronomy 5.

that it may be well with you and that you may
multiply greatly, just as the Lord, the God of your
fathers, has promised you, in a land flowing with
milk and honey.

Hear, O Israel! The Lord is our God, the Lord
is one! And you shall love the Lord your God with
all your heart and with all your soul and with all
your might." (6:1–5)

Parents were to pass down to their children and grandchildren
an awesome and healthy fear of God, an attentive ear to His voice,
and a life of obedience (vv. 2–3a). This kind of all-encompassing
love for God is authentic. You can't fake it. And parents who model
this love will forever impact their children for good.

Regarding the Truth of His Word

For authenticity to be maintained in the home, there must be
a conscious, consistent transfer of God's truth to the young. First,
though, that truth must capture the heart of the parent.

"And these words, which I am commanding you
today, shall be on your heart." (v. 6)

Then a transfer takes place.

"And you shall teach them diligently to your sons."
(v. 7a)

As translated, the word *diligently* is an adverb. But in the Hebrew
text, it is a verb, *shanan,* which means "to sharpen." The particular
form of this verb in Hebrew intensifies the action. The sense, then,
would be: "You shall *intensely* sharpen your sons." The teaching is
not passive but aggressively active. The transfer of truth takes an
investment of time and effort; it isn't automatic.

"And [you] shall talk of them when you sit in your
house and when you walk by the way and when you
lie down and when you rise up." (v. 7b)

What exactly did Moses mean by the word *talk* used here? The
Hebrew has terms for preaching and for lecturing, but Moses uses
neither of these. Instead, the word used simply means "talking." No
formal lecture. No catechism. No rigid routine or Sunday school
structure. Simply talking. Not just on Sunday. And not just at

bedtime. But talking that takes place naturally during all times of the day, every day. Above all else, the home should be a place where God can be comfortably discussed in any conversation, at any time.

Regarding Our Response toward Affluence

Entering Canaan—the land of milk and honey—the Israelites experienced the same temptations we do.

> "Then it shall come about when the Lord your God brings you into the land which He swore to your fathers, Abraham, Isaac and Jacob, to give you, great and splendid cities which you did not build, and houses full of all good things which you did not fill, and hewn cisterns which you did not dig, vineyards and olive trees which you did not plant, and you shall eat and be satisfied, then watch yourself, lest you forget the Lord who brought you from the land of Egypt, out of the house of slavery. You shall fear only the Lord your God; and you shall worship Him, and swear by His name. You shall not follow other gods, any of the gods of the peoples who surround you." (vv. 10–14)

Suddenly, the Israelites would go from wilderness paupers to wealthy princes. Life would no longer be a Spartan diet of manna and quail, but a smorgasbord in the land of milk and honey. Canaan would be a cornucopia of fulfilled dreams. Luxurious homes. Sprawling estates. Botanical gardens. Fertile farmland.

And what is the Lord's advice in the midst of all this affluence? To watch out, lest they forget to honor the Lord as the true source of all their blessings (see James 1:17). That brings us to another essential ingredient to keep family faith authentic: *a tender, humble heart of gratitude for God's provisions.* Observe that God doesn't say, "Don't live in those cities" or "You shouldn't have nice things" or "You shouldn't have it so easy." He merely says, "Watch out."

Regarding the Need for Survival

Deuteronomy 6:20–25 says that to ensure survival for individual families and for the nation as a whole, there must be *frequent stated reminders of God's faithfulness and grace.*

> "When your son asks you in time to come, saying, 'What do the testimonies and the statutes and the judgments mean which the Lord commanded

you?' then you shall say to your son, 'We were slaves to Pharaoh in Egypt; and the Lord brought us from Egypt with a mighty hand. Moreover, the Lord showed great and distressing signs and wonders before our eyes against Egypt, Pharaoh and all his household; and He brought us out from there in order to bring us in, to give us the land which He had sworn to our fathers.' So the Lord commanded us to observe all these statutes, to fear the Lord our God for our good always and for our survival, as it is today. And it will be righteousness for us if we are careful to observe all this commandment before the Lord our God, just as He commanded us."

When you're living authentic lives of faith, your children will be full of questions: "What does the Bible mean? Why do we believe it? Why don't we live like others around us?" And you'll find that the best answers are stated reminders of God's faithfulness and grace—telling your children what God has done in your life.

Looking Up: The Help above Us

Building into our families a faith that is authentic in today's world is challenging. But there is help from above when we are obedient to God in passing on His truth to our children. That truth is for their good . . . and for their survival. It's a matter of life and death, as another father reminded his son in Proverbs 6:20–23:

> My son, observe the commandment of your father,
> And do not forsake the teaching of your mother;
> Bind them continually on your heart;
> Tie them around your neck.
> When you walk about, they will guide you;
> When you sleep, they will watch over you;
> And when you awake, they will talk to you.
> For the commandment is a lamp, and the teaching
>   is light;
> And reproofs for discipline are the way of life.

When they have learned to follow your lead in their relationship with the Lord, they will not only survive—they will send a wave of authenticity rippling through their families as well.

5

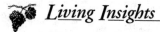

Moses' command is clear and simple. Mom, Dad, teach your children God's Word. What's not so clear or simple is how to teach them.

> Dinner was finished and the dishes pushed aside when Joe brought his Bible from under his chair. He glanced at his wife, Susan, with a look and sigh that meant, Let's try again.
>
> The children around the table groaned a concert of "Oh, no" followed by a solo, "Can we hurry, Dad? I just remembered I have to feed the goldfish."
>
> "Now listen, everybody," Joe said. "I'm going to read about Christ's triumphal entry into Jerusalem." . . .
>
> "Now," he said when he had finished, "let's have some questions. Peter, what did the crowds shout when they saw Jesus riding by?"
>
> Peter, whose mind had no doubt been concentrating on his starving fish, looked blank and finally said, "Dunno, Dad."
>
> Eight-year-old Danny just couldn't remember either.
>
> In an attempt to receive some response, Joe turned to Alisa and asked, "Honey, what did Jesus ride on when he went to Jerusalem?"
>
> Alisa puckered her little mouth in concentration and finally said tentatively, "On a cloud?"[3]

Ever have a devotional like this one? Perhaps it would be better to ask, What parent hasn't?

So what can we do? For some, the answer is to force their children out of anger to attend family devotions. But this often causes resentment and alienates children from a genuine love for God or His Word. Others simply relinquish their responsibility and let the church do it instead. But this short-circuits one of the primary tasks God has given us as parents.

If you feel exasperated or befuddled about how to teach your children spiritual truth, don't give up hope—there is help. Plenty

---

3. Mary White, *Successful Family Devotions* (Colorado Springs, Colo.: NavPress, 1981), p. 9.

of good books, practical ideas, and experienced counsel are available to help you create family devotions that even your children might enjoy. Here are a few excellent resources for starters.

Character Building

Gire, Ken. *Adventures in the Big Thicket*. Pomona, Calif.: Focus on the Family Publishers, 1990. All ages.

————. Kids Praise! Adventure Series. Laguna Hills, Calif.: Kids' Praise Co. of Maranatha Music, 1987–1988. Books and audio cassette tapes are included in this series for four- to seven-year-olds.

McGee and Me! video series. Colorado Springs, Colo.: Focus on the Family; distributed by Tyndale House Publishers. The tapes in this series will appeal to anyone age seven to seventy-seven.

Richmond, Gary. View from the Zoo Series. Dallas, Tex.: Word Publishing, 1990. There are several fun titles in this series of books for six- to nine-year-olds.

Fiction

Gire, Ken. *Treasure in an Oatmeal Box*. Colorado Springs, Colo.: NavPress, 1990. For ages nine to twelve.

Lewis, C. S. The Chronicles of Narnia seven-book set. New York, N.Y.: Macmillan Publishing Co., 1950–56. These classic tales will appeal to nine-year-olds through adults.

Devotional Help

Adventures in Odyssey audio cassette series. Colorado Springs, Colo.: Focus on the Family Publishers; distributed by Word Publishing. This cassettes series is for three- to eleven-year-olds.

Henley, Karyn. *The Beginner's Bible: Timeless Children's Stories*. Sisters, Oreg.: Questar Publishers, 1989. For preschoolers.

Hibbard, Ann. G. T. and the Halo Express Series. Colorado Springs, Colo.: Focus on the Family Publishers; distributed by Word Publishing, 1990. These books in this series will appeal to six- to nine-year-olds.

Lewis, Paul. *Forty Ways to Teach Your Child Values*. Wheaton, Ill.: Tyndale House Publishers, 1985.

Merrill, Dean and Grace. *Together at Home: One Hundred Proven Activities to Nurture Your Children's Faith.* Pomona, Calif.: Focus on the Family Publishers; distributed by Word Publishing, 1988.

Spier, Peter. *Noah's Ark.* New York, N.Y.: Doubleday, 1977. For preschoolers.

White, Mary. *Successful Family Devotions.* Colorado Springs, Colo.: NavPress, 1981.

Williford, Carolyn. *Devotions for Families That Can't Sit Still.* Wheaton, Ill.: Scripture Press Publications, Victor Books, 1990.

Several of these may be available at your local library or church library. For further recommendations, contact your local Christian bookstore, or call Focus on the Family and ask to speak with the Correspondence Department.

 Living Insights

Books, tapes, videos—they are all helpful in teaching our children about the Lord. But the most powerful method of imparting God's truth is with our lives, how we live.

> Ever wonder what kind of impact Jesus' life would have had on the disciples had He only taught them inside a temple for three years? Never any healings, only descriptions of them. Never any real moments of compassion—the woman caught in adultery, the father with a demon-possessed son—only imaginary moments fixed on scrolls of papyrus. Never any excited crowds, sermons on mountainsides, or miracles at tombs. Just the disciples sitting in the same temple seats day after day, listening.
>
> Fortunately, the disciples *saw* Jesus pray. They witnessed Him reaching out to the leper, feeding the hungry, and driving the money changers from the temple. One life rubbing off on others—demonstration.[4]

---

4. From the study guide *Discipleship: Ministry Up Close and Personal*, coauthored by Lee Hough, from the Bible-teaching ministry of Charles R. Swindoll (Fullerton, Calif.: Insight for Living, 1990), p. 51. For further study concerning how Christ taught His spiritual children, see the study guide *Discipleship: Ministry Up Close and Personal* and Robert Coleman's *The Master Plan of Evangelism*.

What are you demonstrating to your children? Have they witnessed you reaching out to the outcast or the hungry? Are they seeing you walk according to the light of God's Word (Ps. 119:105)?

Pause for a moment and carefully consider what your attitudes and actions—not sermons—are teaching your children in the following areas.

The Lord Jesus

_____

_____

Prayer

_____

_____

Knowing and Obeying God's Word

_____

_____

Compassion for the Unsaved, the Poor, the Oppressed

_____

_____

Humility

_____

_____

Servanthood

_____

_____

St. Francis of Assisi reportedly said, "Preach Jesus, and only when necessary, use words." Is your life a living sermon of Christ to your children?

Chapter 2

MASCULINE MODEL OF LEADERSHIP

1 Thessalonians 2:8–12

In his book *Promises to Peter*, Charlie Shedd tells how the title of his message on parenting changed with his experience of fatherhood. In his early years on the speaking circuit, before he was a father, he called it "How to Raise Your Children." People came in droves to hear it. Then Charlie had a child, and it was a while before he gave that message again. When he did, it had a new name: "Some Suggestions to Parents." Two more children and a number of years later, he was calling it "Feeble Hints to Fellow Strugglers." Several years and children later, he seldom gave that talk. But when he did, his theme was "Anyone here got a few words of wisdom?"

It's tough being a dad. It's almost impossible to live up to your own standards, to say nothing of God's. And the toughest thing of all is that, deep inside, every father knows he is leaving an indelible thumbprint on the life of each of his children. Whether he's nuts-and-bolts practical or scrapes the Milky Way with his visionary ideas; whether he's strong and aggressive or weak and passive; whether he's a workaholic or an alcoholic—there's not a dad who doesn't know that his fingerprints are all over his children as he molds and shapes them into the adults they will become.

How can fathers do this carefully and wisely? In this lesson we will take a few tips on parenting from the apostle Paul. We don't know if Paul was ever a father in the literal sense; but in his first letter to the Thessalonians, we see some fatherly characteristics that are well worth emulating.

A Little Background

The first two churches founded in Europe were in Philippi and Thessalonica. When Paul took a trip to Thessalonica, he saw potential in that city and wanted to stay, even though he was pursued and persecuted by unbelievers (see 1 Thess. 2:1–2). For six weeks, he poured himself into that handful of believers, working night and day to establish them in their newborn faith. Although Paul was never to return for another in-depth visit, the Thessalonian believers had captured his heart. So when he later heard about the waves of persecution that threatened to drown their belief, he threw them two life preservers.

He Sent Timothy to Them

Unable to go to them himself, Paul sent his friend Timothy with words of hope and encouragement (3:2).

He Wrote Them a Letter

When Timothy returned with news of their longing for him, Paul wrote them an impassioned letter of exhortation. Pouring through his pen was a wellspring of love from a father's heart.

> But we proved to be gentle among you, as a nursing mother tenderly cares for her own children . . . imploring each one of you as a father would his own children. (2:7, 11b)

"As a . . . mother . . . as a father"—these words appear nowhere else in Paul's writings. And it's from this context of Paul's fatherly heart that we draw some principles of parenting.

Five Guidelines for Good Dads

From Paul's parental language in 2:8–12, we can paint an instructive portrait of a dad with his kids. Let's look at the vivid colors and subtle strokes that make this portrait so striking.

A Fond Affection

The first quality we see is affection:

> Having thus a fond affection for you. (v. 8a)

Paul had at his fingertips half-a-dozen Greek terms he could have used, but he picked a term found only this once in all the New Testament—a term that means "to feel oneself drawn to something or someone." It's a term of endearment taken from the nursery—a term both masculine and tender . . . the picture of a father gently cradling his tiny child.

How often do *we* really express this kind of "fond affection"? It's easy to hug and kiss a baby, even a small child. But as that child grows up, physical affection is often replaced with physical aloofness—which can have some disastrous results. Research shows that sexual promiscuity in a woman can often be traced to a lack of fatherly affection in her childhood and adolescence.[1] So fathers, demonstrate your love—now, before your child starts looking for it elsewhere.

A Transparent Life

For the rest of verse 8 we can glean the second guideline: a transparent life.

> Having thus a fond affection for you, we were well-pleased to impart to you *not only the gospel of God but also our own lives,* because you had become very dear to us. (emphasis added)

Isn't the gospel important? Absolutely! And isn't it enough? Absolutely not!

It's essential that your children hear the gospel if they are to come to know the Savior you love; and it's even better if the Good News comes from your own lips. But they need more than that. They need instruction about life, and they need a father who lets them watch him live it, mistakes and all. They need to see how you handle your finances, how you make decisions, what your values are, and what makes you laugh. They need to hear you admit when you're wrong and see you stand up for your faith. They need to know you inside out—and to feel your interest and belief in them. The word *impart* means "to convey, to contribute, to share fully" . . . with children who know without a doubt that are "very dear" to you.

An Unselfish Diligence

In verse 9, we see Paul hard at work, making sacrifices for the sake of Christ.

> For you recall, brethren, our labor and hardship, how working night and day so as not to be a burden to any of you, we proclaimed to you the gospel of God.

Taking this into a family setting, we can learn the importance of financial responsibility and bearing up under the strain of demands. What an example for your children to see! They don't need

---

1. Dan Benson, *The Total Man* (Wheaton, Ill.: Tyndale House Publishers, 1977), p. 178.

material goods in place of your time. They don't need to see the fruit of their father's labor instead of their father. But they do need to see their dad do a day's work for a day's pay; and they do need opportunities to earn their own way.

A Spiritual Authenticity

We can shade in two important aspects of a father's spiritual responsibility—belief and behavior—from verses 9b–10.

> We proclaimed to you the gospel of God. You are witnesses, and so is God, how devoutly and uprightly and blamelessly we behaved toward you believers.

Too many fathers leave the spiritual aspect of child raising to Mom; if Christ is taught at all, it's usually by the mother. Dads need to teach Christ too, and then live their lives in a way that backs it up.

A Positive Influence

The final stroke on our painting of parenthood is a positive influence.

> You know how we were exhorting and encouraging and imploring each one of you as a father would his own children, so that you may walk in a manner worthy of the God who calls you into His own kingdom and glory. (vv. 11–12)

Dan Benson, in his book *The Total Man*, tells us the results of a disturbing survey: for every single positive statement made in the average home, there are ten negative ones.[2] It's hard to be positive while your kids are maturing. It's part of your job to correct them, right? But children whose ears are full of the words "No" and "Don't" and "Stop that!" learn not to trust their instincts, not to try. Children who hear "That's great!" and "You can do it!" as often as they hear "That's not a good idea" will face new challenges with self-confidence and explore their potential without fear.

2. Benson, *The Total Man*, p. 183.

In Conclusion

Although cement has certain internal properties that determine how it can be shaped, it nevertheless is greatly influenced by the molding of external forces. In the child's case, that molding influence is the parent. Anne Ortlund illustrates this in her book *Children Are Wet Cement*.

> That child of yours is helpless in the hands of the people around him. He is pliable to their shaping; they set his mold. What will he become?
>
> That's what Abraham Lincoln asked—who never paid more than minimum courtesy to the adults whom he passed on the street, but when he passed a child, he stepped out of the way and doffed his hat.
>
> "These adults I know," he said, "but who knows what the children may become?"
>
> These little ones, kicking in their cribs or racing around—they are tomorrow's world, our most precious possession, most powerful potential. . . .
>
> But the awesome thing is that they receive their impressions of life from us—even their impressions of what makes godliness. . . .
>
> Well, they are God's wonderful gift to us. Certainly they make us what we would never be, if they weren't watching us and copying us!
>
> They are the arrows from our bows, with their direction dependent on our guidance.
>
> They are the receivers of our batons, when we begin to tire.
>
> They are tomorrow's heroes and rescuers and achievers—or else tomorrow's thieves and saboteurs and loafers.[3]

3. Anne Ortlund, *Children Are Wet Cement* (Old Tappan, N.J.: Fleming H. Revell Co., 1981), pp. 38–40.

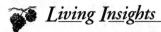

In his book *Making Sense Out of Suffering*, author Peter Kreeft writes,

> I shall never forget reading about the boy in the bubble. . . . He had a rare disease (how common rare diseases seem to be!) that necessitated his living his whole life in a sterile plastic bubble. Any touch, a single germ, could kill him. All communication, recreation, education, everything was through the bubble. Finally, he was dying. Since he was doomed anyway, he asked to touch his father's hand—his father, who had loved him and stayed with him all his life. What unspeakable love and pain was in that one touch![4]

Many children feel like that boy; their whole childhood is spent trapped inside a sterile family bubble void of any physical affection. They, too, ache for the approving touch of their father's hand.

In *How to Really Love Your Child*, Ross Campbell, M.D., emphasizes that giving our children physical affection is *crucial*. For example, young boys up to age seven or eight need to be held, and hugged. Then,

> As a boy grows and becomes older, his need for physical affection such as hugging and kissing lessens but his need for physical contact does not. Instead of primarily "ooey-gooey love stuff," he now wants "boy-style" physical contact such as playful wrestling, jostling, backslapping, playful hitting or boxing, bearhugs, "give-me-five." . . . These ways of making physical contact with a boy are just as genuine a means of giving attention as hugging and kissing. Don't forget that a child *never* outgrows a need for *both* types. . . .
>
> Let's talk about girls and their needs now. . . .
>
> A father helps his daughter to approve of herself by showing her that he himself approves of her. He does this by applying . . . unconditional love, eye

---

4. Peter Kreeft, *Making Sense Out of Suffering* (Ann Arbor, Mich.: Servant Books, 1986), p. 5.

contact, and physical contact, as well as focused attention. A daughter's need for her father to do this begins as early as two years of age. This need, although important at younger ages, becomes greater as the girl grows older and approaches that almost magic age of thirteen.[5]

Dads, the chances are good that many of you had fathers who were culturally conditioned not to show any physical affection. Instead of receiving an affirming hug when you felt rejected or hurt as a child, you were probably told "little boys don't cry" or "be a man, gut it up."

Don't make that same mistake with your children. Don't just tell them you love them or *assume* that they know this simply because you buy them things. Show them. Imitate your Father in heaven who *demonstrated* His love for you through Christ (Rom. 5:8; Eph. 2:4–7).

Oh, what unspeakable love can be communicated, what pain can be eased by your touch.

Take a moment to list the names of your children; then, beside each one, write out some ways to better demonstrate your love through physical affection.

_____ _____

_____

_____

_____ _____

_____

_____

_____ _____

_____

_____

5. Ross Campbell, M.D., *How to Really Love Your Child* (Wheaton, Ill.: Scripture Press Publications, Victor Books, 1977), pp. 47–51.

_____ _____

                               _____

                               _____

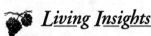 ## Living Insights

Appropriate physical touching is not all that's required of a good father. He must also learn how to exhort and encourage his children with the touch of his words.

Are your words heavy-handed or gentle? Calloused or sensitive? Angry or affirming?

"How many times have I got to tell you? . . . You _never_ get it right. . . . Why can't you be like your brother? . . . That looks ridiculous. . . . Oh, why don't you go live with your mother!"

> Death and life are in the power of the tongue.
> (Prov. 18:21a)

"Get down. . . . Leave that alone. . . . Go away—stop—quit— DON'T! . . . Because I say so!"

> A soothing tongue is a tree of life,
> But perversion in it crushes the spirit. (15:4)

"I love you. . . . I'll help you. . . . How was your day? . . . Mom and I thank God for you. . . . I'm sorry. . . . You did a great job cleaning up your room. . . . Thank you. . . . Please. . . . You go first. . . . I used to fall off my bike a lot too! . . . Your attitude has been really good today."

> Pleasant words are a honeycomb,
> Sweet to the soul and healing to the bones. (16:24)

With your spouse's help, list the encouraging phrases you say most often in routine exchanges at home.

_____

_____

_____

_____

What are some of the hurtful words that need to be weeded out from your family conversations?

_____

_____

_____

_____

_____

> Don't use bad language. Say only what is good and helpful to those you are talking to, and what will give them a blessing. (Eph. 4:29 LB)

Why not make it a family project to print or paint this verse on poster board or newsprint, discuss what it means, have everyone commit to doing it, and then hang it someplace where it will be a visible reminder to all?

Chapter 3

POSITIVE PARTNER
OF SUPPORT

2 Timothy 1:1–7; Proverbs 24:3–4

She cooks, she cleans, she comforts, she corrects. She has six pairs of hands, and eyes in the back of her head. *Mother.*

For some, this word conjures up images of June Cleaver, complete with lace apron and pearls—singing lullabies, baking brownies, kissing away a child's hot tears. Others envision the Erma Bombeck model, who drives a wood-paneled station wagon and whose hobby is dust. Whatever the type, no one has more influence than a mother. For better or worse, she will forever impact the life of her child.

Tough and tender, wise and warm, a mother must be all things to all her family . . . at all times. That's quite a job description, and anyone who is a mother or has watched one in action knows there's no career more demanding . . . or more endangered in today's society. In this lesson, let's look at the increasingly rare qualities of mothering that are essential to building and preserving the home.

A Firm Foundation

Tools a Mother Needs

All homes must be built on a firm foundation. In Proverbs 24:3–4 we see the tools needed to establish a rock-solid home.

> By wisdom a house is built,
> And by understanding it is established;
> And by knowledge the rooms are filled
> With all precious and pleasant riches.

Solomon is suggesting that homes are built with three primary tools: *wisdom, understanding,* and *knowledge.* Wisdom is the ability to see with discernment, to view life through God's eyes. Understanding is the skill of responding with insight, reading between the lines. Knowledge learning with perception—having a teachable spirit, a willingness to learn. Even from our children.

These tools have nothing to do with hammer and nails or trowel and mortar. They are relational. And Mom, you can have all three. With God-given wisdom, understanding, and knowledge, you can be filling the rooms of your home with a rich heritage of godly character traits, deep relationships, and lasting memories.

A story is told of four men arguing over the best translation of the Bible. The first man liked the King James Version because of its beautiful, eloquent English. Another insisted that the New American Standard Bible was best because of its accuracy to the original text. A third preferred Moffatt for its quaint, penetrating words and captivating phrases. After pondering the issue, the fourth man said, "Personally, I have always preferred my mother's translation." Tolerating the others' chuckles, he responded, "Yes, she translated it. She translated each page of the Bible into life. It is the most convincing translation I ever saw."

A New Testament Example

The New Testament shows us a mother who used the tools of wisdom, understanding, and knowledge in rearing her son Timothy. Although we don't know much about Timothy's mother, we do know that she and his grandmother made an incredible investment in his spiritual life. So much so that Paul, the wise apostle, was drawn to the young man, forging a fifteen-year friendship with him. As Paul lay dying in a Roman dungeon, Timothy was the friend he sought out.

> Paul, an apostle of Jesus Christ . . . to Timothy, my beloved son. . . .
> I thank God, whom I serve with a clear conscience the way my forefathers did, as I constantly remember you in my prayers night and day, longing to see you. (2 Tim. 1:1–4a)

Looking back on their friendship, Paul is filled with gratitude and good memories. In the verses that follow, we'll discover the qualities that made Timothy unique and appealing, qualities he learned from his mother.

A Mother's Contributions

In verses 4–7 we find five distinct contributions a mother can make to the family, filling each room with her motherly touch until her house becomes a home.

Transparent Tenderness

Paul first mentions Timothy's tears.

> Even as I recall your tears, so that I may be filled with joy. (v. 4b)

Paul remembers Timothy's tenderness, a trait likely passed down from his mother. In fact, most of us learned tenderness from our mothers, while our dads taught us diligence. From Dad we learned the value of a dollar, the significance of honesty, the importance of standing alone when everything turns against us. But we learned transparent tenderness from Mom.

Mother, don't lose that quality—it's one of your greatest contributions to your family. Your warm embrace, eager smile, and soft reply will be a safe harbor for the child who's tossed and battered by life's stormy seas.

Authentic Spirituality

In verse 5 Paul refers directly to Timothy's heritage, his roots.

> For I am mindful of the sincere faith within you, which first dwelt in your grandmother Lois, and your mother Eunice, and I am sure that it is in you as well.

The Greek term for sincere is *anupokritos*, which means "unhypocritical." Nothing phony here; it's real, lived-out faith. Paul knew the sincere faith modeled in Mama Eunice and Grandma Lois had impacted Timothy (see also 3:14–15). That's the way authentic spirituality works. Christian churches, schools, and friends can give children the facts, the words to say. But those words won't fit reality unless God's truth is translated at home.

Inner Confidence

> And for this reason I remind you to kindle afresh the gift of God which is in you through the laying on of my hands. For God has not given us a spirit of timidity, but of *power* . . . (1:6–7a, emphasis added)

In the Greek, *power* has in mind "inherent strength" and "inner might."[1] Notice that timidity is not a desirable trait—it's a synonym

---

1. The Greek word is *dunamis*, from which we get our words *dynamic* and *dynamite*.

for insecurity or inferiority. It's amazing how your children can sense your own attitude toward yourself—and how they will emulate it, good or bad. One of the reasons Timothy stayed true to the Scriptures and stood strong in his ministry was because he had learned inner confidence from his mother.

Mom, do you know that God wants to use you to build healthy self-esteem in your child? Note these words from family expert and psychologist Dr. James Dobson:

> It is a wise adult who understands that self-esteem is the most fragile characteristic in human nature, and once broken, its reconstruction is more difficult than repairing Humpty Dumpty. . . .
>
> . . . Although our task is more difficult for some children than for others, there *are* ways to teach a child of his genuine significance, regardless of the shape of his nose or the size of his ears or the efficiency of his mind. *Every* child is entitled to hold up his head, not in haughtiness and pride, but in confidence and security. This is the concept of human worth intended by our Creator. How foolish for us to doubt our value when He formed us in His own image! . . .
>
> . . . When the child is convinced that he is greatly loved and respected by his parents, he is inclined to accept his own worth as a person.[2]

Inner confidence, like transparent tenderness and authentic spirituality, is passed down from generation to generation . . . as in Timothy's life, from grandmother to mother to son. How's your self-esteem, Mom? Are you taking the time to cultivate a positive self-image in your child?

Unselfish Love

Verse 7a continues with another gift from God—a gift everyone, and especially mothers, can emulate.

> For God has not given us a spirit of timidity, but of power and *love* . . . (emphasis added)

2. James Dobson, *Hide or Seek*, rev. ed. (Old Tappan, N.J.: Fleming H. Revell Co., 1979), pp. 57, 60, 62.

This kind of love—*agapē*—seeks the highest good of the other person. It needs to be evident in every facet of your life, Mom. And your love shows through in two ways especially. First, in your sense of humor—when you laugh in the midst of pressure and refuse to take yourself too seriously, which gives your child a more positive and unthreatening environment to grow in. And second, in your sense of insight—when you listen to hurts and hear what isn't said, showing your child that you care and want to help.

In another letter, this time to the Corinthians, Paul devoted an entire chapter to the subject of unselfish love (1 Cor. 13). One mother has written a paraphrase that aptly describes this essential ingredient of mothering.

> If I talk to my children about what is right and what is wrong, but have not love, I am like a ringing doorbell or pots banging in the kitchen. And though I know what stages they will go through, and understand their growing pains, and can answer all their questions about life, and believe myself to be a devoted mother, but have not love, I am nothing.
>
> If I give up the fulfillment of a career to make my children's lives better, and stay up all night sewing costumes or baking cookies on short notice, but grumble about lack of sleep, I have not love and accomplish nothing.
>
> A loving mother is patient with her children's immaturity and kind even when they are not; a loving mother is not jealous of their youth nor does she hold it over their heads whenever she has sacrificed for them. A loving mother does not push her children into doing things her way. She is not irritable, when the chicken pox have kept her confined with three whining children for two weeks, and does not resent the child who brought the affliction home in the first place.
>
> A loving mother is not relieved when her disagreeable child finally disobeys her directly and she can punish him, but rather rejoices with him when he is being more cooperative. A loving mother bears much of the responsibility for her children; she believes in them; she hopes in each one's individual ability to stand out as a light in a dark world; she endures

every backache and heartache to accomplish that.

A loving mother never really dies. As for home-baked bread, it will be consumed and forgotten; as for spotless floors, they will soon gather dust and heelmarks. And as for children, well, right now toys, friends, and food are all-important to them. But when they grow up it will have been how their mother loved them that will determine how they love others. In that way she will live on.

So care, training, and a loving mother reside in a home, these three, but the greatest of these is a loving mother.[3]

Self-control

Take a final look at 2 Timothy 1:7.

> For God has not given us a spirit of timidity, but of power and love and *discipline*. (emphasis added)

Good moms balance tenderness and love with discipline. They set parameters and know when it's time to say, "That's it; that's enough." In his excellent book *Hide or Seek*, James Dobson tells the story of a research project conducted by Dr. Stanley Cooper-smith, associate professor of psychology at the University of California. After studying 1,738 middle-class boys and their families over a number of years, Coopersmith identified three important differences between the families of boys with high self-esteem and those with low self-worth.

First, *the high-esteem children were more loved and appreciated at home.* Their parents' love was deep and real; their words had substance.

Second, and perhaps most revealing, *the high-esteem group had parents whose approach to discipline was significantly more strict.* They taught self-control. In contrast, the parents of the low-esteem group were much more permissive, creating a sense of insecurity. These boys were more likely to feel that no one cared enough to enforce the rules.

Third, *the high-esteem group had homes that were characterized by democracy and open communication.* Once boundaries had been

---

3. Dianne Lorang, as quoted in *Keep the Fire Glowing*, by Pat Williams, Jill Williams, and Jerry Jenkins (Old Tappan, N.J.: Fleming H. Revell Co., 1986), pp. 152–53.

established, the boys had the freedom to ask questions and express themselves in an environment of acceptance.[4]

Mom, don't underestimate the value of teaching self-control. In your discipline, you are building your children's character, enhancing their self-esteem, and helping them learn to be responsible for themselves.

A Return to Our Foundation

How do mothers build solid homes? First they secure the foundation. Remember the tools?

> By *wisdom* a house is built,
> And by *understanding* it is established;
> And by *knowledge* the rooms are filled
> With all precious and pleasant riches.
> (Prov. 24:3–4, emphasis added)

Those riches are transparent tenderness, authentic spirituality, inner confidence, unselfish love, and self-control. Children see what God's love is all about through their parents, especially their mothers, since they spend the most time with them. Mom, when you laugh, your children hear God laugh. When you cry, they see Him cry.

Never doubt the value of your role. Without your positive, supportive partnership, the family could not survive.

🍇 *Living Insights*

Wisdom . . . understanding . . . discernment.

These basic tools that build, establish, and fill a home with precious and pleasant riches have *time* written all over them. It takes time to develop these qualities in ourselves and in our relationships with our children.

The trend in motherhood today, however, is away from the skillful use of such time-consuming tools. Mothers are instead being pressured to pursue lifestyles that focus their time and attention outside the home.

---

4. Dobson, *Hide or Seek*, pp. 92–93.

Dolores Curran writes:

> In an incisive article called "Fast Folk," which appeared in . . . *Harpers*, Louis T. Grant dissects an article published earlier in *Woman's Day* in which the life-style of one working mother is praised and presented as a model of sorts. Listen to this woman's life. She rushes from home to work in the morning, eating yogurt in the car for breakfast; has lunch at the spa where she works out; leaves child care to her husband, who also has a managerial position forty miles the other side of home; pilots a small plane in her leisure time for pleasure; teaches on the side a class at a local women's college; leaves the kids with Grandma; leaves the kids with sitters; leaves the kids. . . . Grant likens this life-style, which he calls "fast folk," to keeping up with the gerbils. In his immensely perceptive piece, he illustrates the shallowness of relationships in a fast-folk family. There's no time in such a family for one another, for intimacy, for communication, for listening. That's for slowpokes. And, the author points out, "children are slowpokes."[5]

Mom, is yours a fast-folk lifestyle? Do your priorities reflect a commitment to building your home with wisdom, establishing it with understanding, and filling its rooms with the riches of knowledge? For the next few moments, perform an on-site inspection of the foundation you're laying in your children's lives.

1. *Wisdom:* How am I modeling the ability to see life through God's eyes? What else could I be doing to teach this?

_____

_____

_____

_____

5. Dolores Curran, *Traits of a Healthy Family* (Minneapolis, Minn.: Winston Press, 1983), pp. 117–18.

2. *Understanding*: Am I able to respond with insight because I'm intimately acquainted with God's Word and my children? Am I taking the time and effort to skillfully apply the tool of understanding—reading between the lines—or am I simply hammering them into conformity with terse, angry commands?

_____

_____

_____

3. *Knowledge*: How perceptive am I of the way my children feel and think? How are they different from each other, spiritually and temperamentally?

_____

_____

_____

In addition to shaping your children's characters, these basic tools will also create precious and pleasant memories that will influence them long after you're gone.

Why not gather your children together some evening and have everyone, Mom and Dad included, relate a special memory of the family and tell why it means so much to them. It might give you tremendous insight into how to better apply the tools of wisdom, understanding, and knowledge.

Living Insights

"Well, that's the way we always did it in my family." Ever heard that one? Sure you have. Most of us have even said it a time or two—or twenty. It's what we instinctively say when we're trying to resolve an issue in which there's no clear-cut principle or plan to tell us what to do.

Take Christmas, for example. His family opened presents on Christmas Eve after the midnight service. Her family *always* opened them on Christmas morning, sipping a steamy cup of wassail and listening to Bing croon about a white Christmas. But his family never did like Bing Crosby. Well, she doesn't like the smell of incense at 12:30 in the morning. He *does*. She *doesn't!* Him: "Fine!

We'll just take all our presents back and skip Christmas." Her: "That's just fine with me!"

We can all grin about this because we know what it's like when two that's-the-way-we-always-did-its collide head on. More than just two people, you have two sets of parents, two families, two totally different backgrounds suddenly slamming into each other. And what set these two powerful trains in motion? What determined the course they would take? The home. The home is *the* most potent influence in our lives—especially when we're young. What children live with, as Dorothy Law Nolte points out, they learn.

> If a child lives with criticism,
> he learns to condemn.
> If a child lives with hostility,
> he learns to fight.
> If a child lives with ridicule,
> he learns to be shy.
> If a child lives with shame,
> he learns to feel guilty.
> If a child lives with tolerance,
> he learns to be patient.
> If a child lives with encouragement,
> he learns to have confidence.
> If a child lives with praise,
> he learns appreciation.
> If a child lives with fairness,
> he learns justice.
> If a child lives with security,
> he learns to have faith.
> If a child lives with approval,
> he learns to like himself.
> If a child lives with acceptance and friendship,
> he learns to find love in the world.[6]

Mom, what are your children living with? Transparent tenderness? Authentic spirituality? Inner confidence? Unselfish love? Self-control? Set aside some time to pray about the kinds of godly character traits they will naturally exhibit because "that's the way it was always done" at home.

---

6. Dorothy Law Nolte, as quoted in *Children Are Wet Cement*, by Anne Ortlund (Old Tappan, N.J.: Fleming H. Revell Co., 1981), p. 58.

Chapter 4

YOUR BABY HAS THE BENTS
(PART ONE)
Proverbs 22:6

Most parents view the cooing bundle of baby fat they bring home from the maternity ward as a cuddly lump of clay, soft and completely pliable in their hands. They believe they can take the personality of their baby, squeeze it, roll it, mold it into any shape they desire, pop it into a kiln until it's good and hard, and send it out to face the world.

But that perception of child rearing fails to take into account the inherent properties of the clay itself. Those characteristics determine, to a large extent, how it can be shaped and how it will respond to the kiln. Likewise, although the personality of the child can be influenced by the hands of the parent, the preestablished characteristics of the child determine how and to what extent it can be molded.

In today's lesson we'll take a look at Proverbs 22:6, a key passage in discovering and developing those inborn characteristics.

> Train up a child in the way he should go,
> Even when he is old he will not depart from it.

As integral as this verse is to raising children, few parents understand what it really says.

The Popular Interpretation of Proverbs 22:6

Many see this verse as saying that if children have been carted off to church every Sunday, made to read the Bible each day, instructed to memorize Scripture, taught to read only Christian books and see only Christian films, then those children will stay on the straight and narrow path. And, even if they do play the prodigal and morally journey into some distant country, at some point they will come to their senses and get back on course.

As popular as this interpretation is, it doesn't always square with experience. Real life teaches us that not all prodigals come home. The bottom of the ocean is strewn with the wreckage of ships that have strayed from their course and never returned safely to harbor.

Sadly, our memories, too, are strewn with the shipwrecked lives of loved ones who charted courses onto the high seas, rode immorality's crest—and sank.

The Proper Interpretation of Proverbs 22:6

Not only does the popular interpretation of Proverbs 22:6 not square experientially, it doesn't square exegetically.

The Nature of the Training

Let's begin by looking at the words *train up*. The Hebrew term behind this phrase originally referred to the palate or the roof of the mouth. It was used to describe the action of a midwife who, soon after a child's birth, would dip her fingers into a juice made from crushed dates and massage the infant's gums and palate. This tangy taste created a sensation for sucking. Then she would place the child in the mother's arms to begin nursing.[1] Likewise, parents are to create a thirst for the nourishing flow of their wisdom and counsel.

The Duration of the Training

The word *child* invariably calls to mind a little one somewhere between infancy and four or five years of age. However, the Scriptures use this term in a broader sense, ranging anywhere from a newborn to a person of marriageable age.[2] The point is that the principle applies to any dependent child still living under the parents' roof.

The Implementation of the Training

The manner of training is suggested by the word *in*, which means "in keeping with, in cooperation with, in accordance to something." The literal rendering of "in the way he should go" is "according to his way." That's altogether different from *your* way, *your* plan, *your* curriculum. The verse doesn't mean to train up a child as you see him. Rather, if you want your training to be meaningful and wise,

---

1. The word was also used for breaking a wild horse by placing a rope in its mouth, thereby bringing it into submission.

2. Although translated differently at times, the same Hebrew word for *child* is used in many different passages. For example, in 1 Samuel 4:21 the term *boy* is used of a newborn infant. In Exodus 2:2–3 *child* is used to describe three-month-old Moses. In 1 Samuel 1:22 it is used of Samuel before he was weaned. In Genesis 21:12–20 *lad* is used to refer to Ishmael, a preteen. In Genesis 37:2 *youth* is used of Joseph at age 17. And in Genesis 34:19 *young man* is used of a boy of marriageable age.

be observant and discover your *child's* way, and adapt your training accordingly.

Strengthening this idea is the word *way*.[3] Notice its use in Proverbs 30:18–19.

> There are three things which are too wonderful
> for me,
> Four which I do not understand:
> The way of an eagle in the sky,
> The way of a serpent on a rock,
> The way of a ship in the middle of the sea,
> And the way of a man with a maid.

The Hebrew term for *way* literally means "road" or "path." In a figurative sense, it means a characteristic. In Proverbs 22:6, the underlying idea is that the child's characteristics are preformed by God, distinct and set. The word *bent* describes the infant's personality perfectly.[4] Each child is not a totally pliable lump of clay but has certain bents prescribed according to a predetermined pattern. And these bents greatly affect how the child should be handled and how moldable the child will be.

Think of it this way: Each child is hand-stitched by the Lord— not mass-manufactured in some sweatshop. For instance, the mind is intricately woven with the finest of neurological threads. The emotions are given a distinct texture, with a feel all their own. The personality is cut from a unique bolt of cloth. Like snowflakes and fingerprints, no two are alike.

Consider the radical differences in these Old Testament brothers: Cain and Abel . . . Solomon and Absalom . . . even Jacob and Esau, who were twins, demonstrated significant physical and psychological differences.

Now consider your children. How different each one is. How distinct—physically, mentally, emotionally, spiritually. God wants you to know your children, to appreciate the unique way they are crafted, and to train them according to their specific characteristics.

---

3. In Hebrew the noun form is *derek*; the verb form is *darak*.

4. The basic concept behind the verb *darak* has to do with setting foot on territory or objects. In Psalm 7:12 the word is used of God who "has bent His bow and made it ready." That is, He has set His foot on the bow in order to bend it and string it. In a similar way, God puts His foot on the physical, psychological, and personality bows of our lives to bend them in specific ways.

As parents, we must be careful to avoid two errors: first, rearing our children the way we were reared—mistakes and all; and second, comparing our children with each other and applying the same approach to all. Both errors stem from a failure to understand and appreciate how fearfully and wonderfully each is made.

The Results of the Training

The latter portion of Proverbs 22:6 states that "when he is old he will not depart from it." The root meaning of the Hebrew word for *old* is "hair on the chin." It suggests someone approaching adulthood, not retirement. Solomon is not envisioning a ninety-year-old prodigal returning home. He's thinking of a boy who's just starting to grow a beard. Thus, when the child reaches maturity, he will not depart from the way in which he has been trained.

The Parental Application of Proverbs 22:6

Two questions arise for the parent intent on applying this passage of Scripture: How can I know my child's bents? And, What are those bents, so I can nurture them? We'll answer the first question now and the second one in the next chapter. If we look closely at Proverbs 20:11–13, the answer to the first question will come into focus.

> It is by his deeds that a lad distinguishes himself
> If his conduct is pure and right.
> The hearing ear and the seeing eye,
> The Lord has made both of them.
> Do not love sleep, lest you become poor;
> Open your eyes, and you will be satisfied with food.

Taking these pieces of counsel together, we are to observe our children and how we are to observe them—with diligence. We shouldn't let our eyes droop or sleep. We must be alert to how our children respond to life situations. Basically that takes two things—time and concentration.

Your children *are* making themselves known. The question is, are you noticing? If you're beginning to feel that you don't really know or understand them, now is the best time to start. You don't need a degree in theology . . . or a Ph.D. in psychology . . . or even an uncommon portion of common sense. All you need is a sensitive spirit. And you can start right now, simply by asking God to begin making you more sensitive to the unique qualities He has created in your children.

🍇 *Living Insights* _____

All parents make mistakes in raising their children. Mistakes like the one Russell Baker remembers in *Growing Up*, his hilarious autobiography about his boyhood.

> An evening when [Uncle Jack], my mother, Aunt Pat, and I were in the kitchen, the conversation came around to a neighbor who had just had a baby. I made the mistake of saying something that indicated I was curious about where babies came from. Uncle Jack looked at my mother.
>
> "Doesn't he know about *that* yet?" he asked.
>
> No, she said, she hadn't gotten around to *that* yet. "Why don't I take him upstairs and tell him?" he suggested.
>
> She must have felt an immense sense of relief. "I think it's about time somebody did," she said.
>
> Uncle Jack looked at me gravely. "Go upstairs," he said. "There's something I want to talk to you about alone."
>
> I went. I was in a dreadful state of mind. The awful moment had come at last. I was going to be told "the facts of life." . . .
>
> Uncle Jack was slow in arriving, and, when he finally did come up, he didn't seem to be too easy in his own mind. He looked at me and then walked across the room and looked out the window. Then he paced silently for a minute or two.
>
> Finally: "You think the Giants can win the pennant this year?" he asked.
>
> "Well, they've got Carl Hubbell, who's the best pitcher in the League, and Mel Ott hits .350, and if . . ."[5]

5. Russell Baker, *Growing Up* (New York, N.Y.: New American Library, 1982), pp. 167–68.

Baseball. Now that was something Uncle Jack was comfortable talking about. And he did, until the two of them finally exhausted the subject.

> Uncle Jack went back to the window and looked out again, then turned to face me.
> "Look here," he said, "you know how babies are made, don't you?"
> "Sure," I said.
> "Well that's all there is to it," he said.
> "I know that," I said.
> "I thought you did," he said.
> "Sure," I said.
> "Let's go on back downstairs," he said.
> We went downstairs together.
> "Did you tell him?" my mother asked.
> "Everything," Uncle Jack said.[6]

You can't help but laugh at such a comical and common parenting mistake as this one. Your grandparents probably made this mistake, the same as your parents probably did and you might—unless you change.

For the next few minutes, write down the particular child-rearing mistakes your parents made that you want to avoid with your children.

_____

_____

_____

_____

_____

_____

_____

_____

6. Baker, Growing Up, p. 168.

Most of us don't have any problem identifying the mistakes our parents made. It's learning how to be better parents ourselves that is the real challenge. With each mistake that you listed, go back now and write what you have done or need to do in order to keep this same mistake from being repeated.

_____

_____

_____

_____

_____

_____

_____

_____

_____

_____

Living Insights

Isn't it interesting how we can live with people for a long time and still not really know them? Some of us have trouble remembering the color of our children's eyes, much less the makeup of their characters. To be sure this isn't describing you, why not pause and write a composite sketch of each of your children's physical, mental, emotional, and spiritual traits. You might want to do this on a separate sheet of paper so you can exchange evaluations with your spouse, if possible, and learn from each other's perspective about the unique bents God has given your children.

One more thing—save what you write! These will be fun for both you and your children to look back on in the years to come.

Chapter 5

YOUR BABY HAS THE BENTS
(PART TWO)
Psalm 139:1–3, 13–16; 51:5

Raising children is a lot like baking a cake—if you don't follow the recipe, you won't realize it until it's too late!

In baking, it is essential to use the proper ingredients in the proper amounts. Yet in a busy kitchen, it's easy to skim over the directions and confuse a tablespoon with a teaspoon or baking soda with baking powder. It's easy, too, in the interest of economy, to make a few compromises. To substitute shortening for butter. Or imitation vanilla for the real thing.

But too many compromises and too many miscalculations could leave you with a mess on your hands—both in the kitchen and in your children's lives.

Today we'll review a recipe Proverbs 22:6 gives for raising a child. Then we'll take a look at a few more ingredients from the bountiful cupboards of the Psalms.

Review of Foundational Information

Proverbs 22:6 implies that we need to *know* our child, to familiarize ourselves with the distinct ingredients God has placed within that little package of a person. This is the primary task of parenting.

> Train up a child in the way he should go,
> Even when he is old he will not depart from it.

We might paraphrase the verse to read: "Adapt the training of your children so that it is in keeping with their individual gifts or *bents*—the God-given characteristics built into them at birth. When maturity comes, they will not leave the training they have received." Two significant observations arise from this verse.

A Child's Characteristics Are Built-in

A child is not a soft lump of dough that we can shape into anything we want if we just exert enough pressure. On the contrary, each child is deposited into our arms as a package of presifted, premeasured ingredients—ingredients that determine whether the child will turn out as a cake or a loaf of bread. This leads us to a second observation.

Parental Sensitivity to Those Characteristics Is Vital

Discovering those ingredients is the most essential task of parenting. This requires a great deal of sensitivity. Proverbs 20:11a says that a child's character will make itself known by its actions. Yet parents must be diligent in observing their children in order to cooperate with the right bents and correct the wrong bents in their character (vv. 12–13).

Parenting requires enormous amounts of patience, time, energy, and concentration. And unless the parent gets actively involved in the process, the child's whole future will be impaired.

> The rod and reproof give wisdom,
> But a child who gets his own way brings shame to
> his mother. (29:15)

Literally, the latter half of the verse means, "a child *left to himself* brings shame to his mother." Passive parenting is like passive farming. Without diligent cultivation, we can expect little more than a harvest of weeds.

Knowledge of Internal Bents

All this raises a very practical question: What are *my* child's bents? These internal characteristics are not spelled out in Scripture, but we are given some guidelines as to what they might include. In every child there are bents toward good as well as evil. Let's look first at Psalm 139 to examine the good bents; then we'll go to Psalm 58 to examine the bad.

Toward Good

Psalm 139 is one of the most magnificent of the ancient hymns. It revolves around God: His knowledge of all things (vv. 1–6), His presence in all places (vv. 7–12), His power over all things (vv. 13–16), and His redemptive scrutiny (vv. 23–24). Notice how David describes God's intimate knowledge of his life.

> O Lord, Thou hast searched me and known me.
> Thou dost know when I sit down and when I rise up;
> Thou dost understand my thought from afar.
> Thou dost scrutinize my path and my lying down,

And art intimately acquainted with all my ways.
(vv. 1–3)

God knows us long before our parents do. And His knowledge is not superficial, but it searches to the depths of our being. He knows all our bents, even the most intricate. How could that be? Because He works in the darkness of a tiny womb, delicately fashioning His *magnum opus*, the most regal of all His creative work— a human being.

For Thou didst form my inward parts;
Thou didst weave me in my mother's womb. (v. 13)

Like a fiber-optic camera exploring the womb, the Creator takes us on a guided tour of the developing fetus.[1] The word *Thou* in verse 13 is placed first in the Hebrew sentence to emphasize its importance: "Thou" and none other—not Mother Nature, not chance, not fate—"didst form my inward parts." The verb *form* means "originated or created." And *inward parts* is literally "kidneys," which the Hebrews used to represent the vital organs, including the lungs, heart, brain, and liver. The image in the second part of verse 13 conveys the idea of knitting something together. With that embryonic ball of yarn, God knits together each child. It is no small wonder that David bursts into praise in verse 14.

I will give thanks to Thee, for I am fearfully and
wonderfully made;
Wonderful are Thy works,
And my soul knows it very well.

David continues the anatomy lesson in verse 15.

My frame was not hidden from Thee,
When I was made in secret,
And skillfully wrought in the depths of the earth.

The word *frame* means "bony substance," another way of saying skeleton.[2] The term *skillfully wrought* has a beautiful Hebrew meaning,

---

1. Some stunning examples of fiber-optic photography that display life developing within the womb and illustrate Psalm 139 can be found in the book *A Child Is Born*, by Lennart Nilsson (New York, N.Y.: Delacorte Press, 1977).

2. In the fascinating book *Fearfully and Wonderfully Made*, the surgeon who coauthored the book wrote these words about our frame: "In comparison [to bone], wood can withstand

which can be seen in Exodus where the Tabernacle curtains are described. They were variegated, like a multicolored tapestry, and embroidered like fine needlepoint. The next phrase speaks of "the depths of the earth." This is a poetic way of describing the womb by comparing it to the darkened caverns below the earth's surface. Seen as such, the womb is a place of concealment and protection. Continuing, David shows that God plans our lives, which He so diligently fashions in the cover of darkness.

> Thine eyes have seen my unformed substance;
> And in Thy book they were all written,
> The days that were ordained for me,
> When as yet there was not one of them. (v. 16)

Unformed substance is used in the Talmud to indicate every kind of unshaped material, like a block of wood or a lump of clay. When applied to a human vessel, it would be equivalent to the embryo.

But the phrase "Thine eyes have seen my unformed substance" means something far more than God sitting in the grandstands and spectating while the child develops. The word *seen* means "watched over." It is used in an active sense, like an architect who painstakingly watches over every detail of construction to make sure the builders adhere to the blueprints. The bents in a child's blueprint —at least the good ones—are designed by God, and He oversees their placement during the gestation period. So much so that even the very days of the child are delineated.

Are you watching over your children to discover their bents with the same diligence that God took in His design? Are you studying the architecture of their physical and psychological makeup, looking for God's blueprint and appreciating each strategically placed detail in their personality? Or have you ignored the existing structure and begun a building project of your own, with your own blueprints in mind?

---

even less pulling tension, and could not possibly bear the compression forces that bone can. A wooden pole for the vaulter would quickly snap. Steel, which can absorb both forces well, is three times the weight of bone and would burden us down. The economical body takes this stress-bearing bone and hollows it out, using a weight-saving architectural principle it took people millennia to discover; it then fills the vacant space in the center with an efficient red blood cell factory that turns out a trillion new cells per day. Bone sheathes life." Dr. Paul Brand and Philip Yancey, *Fearfully and Wonderfully Made* (Grand Rapids, Mich.: Zondervan Publishing House, 1980), p. 70.

The sovereign Architect of heaven has given you a sacred and unique creation—that special child you have for only a limited time. Make the most of that time, won't you? Get started on the right foundation, and get to know the child God has so graciously entrusted to your custodial care. Now that we have seen the tremendous care God has taken in making our children unique, how do we go about discovering the good bents He's placed in these little works of art? What are some things to look for?

Since we are created in His image and likeness (Gen. 1:26–27), we are endowed with such traits as intelligence, creativity, a desire to love and be loved, imagination, memory, and feelings. He's also given each of us certain talents, gifts, and aptitudes. And, because we are the work of His hands, we have a built-in longing for Him . . . a spiritual bent. All of these are gifts from God, preformed by Him, and shaped differently to create the uniqueness of each child. Take a moment to consider the truth in Ulrich Schaffer's poem "The Completeness of This Child."

> i am amazed
> at the completeness of this child
> nothing is missing
> this is a person like i am
>
> there is a richness of emotion
> a struggling with the will
> a facing of anxiety
> abandonment in joy
> a life full of hope and failure
> of disappointment and joy
> a life not different from my own
>
> the doubts and fears of being loved or not
> can hurt and kill at three or ten or thirty
> the danger is
> that in looking back
> we laugh at what we thought
> when we were small
> and then transfer those laughs
> to children in our life
> who might be living at the limits of their lives . . .
>
> i have to take more seriously
> each phase of growth

and learn to live inside the head
that feels and doubts and questions

i have to remind myself
that to a child
life is just as big
as it is to me[3]

Let's learn to study our children in order to nurture their good
bents. Because to miss them is like getting a beautiful present from
God . . . and never bothering to unwrap it.

Toward Evil

Coined in the image of God, the child bears a certain imprint
of divinity. But that coin also bears the defacing effects of the Fall.
Like Midas in reverse, Adam's touch on us all has turned the luster
of God's image into tarnish (Rom. 5:12). Psalm 51:5 underscores
this bent toward evil.

Behold, I was brought forth in iniquity,
And in sin my mother conceived me.

David is not saying that the act of conception is evil, but that
at the time of birth he possessed a sinful nature. Psalm 58:2–5
touches on this idea.

No, in heart you work unrighteousness;
On earth you weigh out the violence of your hands.
The wicked are estranged from the womb;
These who speak lies go astray from birth.
They have venom like the venom of a serpent;
Like a deaf cobra that stops up its ear,
So that it does not hear the voice of charmers,
Or a skillful caster of spells.

Note the fateful words *from the womb*. From the very inception
of life, sin is inbred into human nature. Like a serpent, our nature
is full of deadly poison. And like a cobra, it is deaf to reproof.

No matter how cute and cuddly that little baby is in your arms,
it is not free from sin—childhood innocence shouldn't be confused

---

3. Excerpt from "The Completeness of This Child" in *For the Love of Children*, by Ulrich
Schaffer. © 1980 by Ulrich Schaffer. Reprinted by permission of HarperCollins, Publishers, Inc.

with moral purity. The Adamic bent is vividly illustrated in the history of humankind and even more clearly set forth in Scripture.

> "There is none righteous, not even one;
> There is none who understands,
> There is none who seeks for God;
> All have turned aside, together they have become
>   useless;
> There is none who does good,
> There is not even one."
> "Their throat is an open grave,
> With their tongues they keep deceiving,"
> "The poison of asps is under their lips."
> (Rom. 3:10b–13)

The only antidote to sin's poison is counteraction, on both a divine and a human level. Divine help is needed to bring the child to a saving knowledge of Christ; human help is needed to discipline the child. Remember Proverbs 29:15?

> The rod and reproof give wisdom,
> But a child who gets his own way brings shame to
>   his mother.

A Point to Ponder

Just as physical characteristics are hereditary, so the personal characteristics of the parents are passed down generation after generation. Two contrasting cases in point are worthy of our attention:

> "The father of Jonathan Edwards was a minister and his mother was the daughter of a clergyman. Among their descendants were fourteen presidents of colleges, more than one hundred college professors, more than one hundred lawyers, thirty judges, sixty physicians, more than a hundred clergymen, missionaries and theology professors, and about sixty authors. There is scarcely any great American industry that has not had one of his family among its chief promoters. Such is the product of one American Christian family, reared under the most favorable conditions. The contrast is presented in the Jukes family, which could not be made to study and

would not work, and is said to have cost the state of New York a million dollars. Their entire record is one of pauperism and crime, insanity and imbecility. Among their twelve hundred known descendants, three hundred ten were professional paupers, four hundred forty were physically wrecked by their own wickedness, sixty were habitual thieves, one hundred thirty were convicted criminals, fifty-five were victims of impurity, only twenty learned a trade (and ten of these learned it in a state prison), and this notorious family produced seven murderers."[4]

What qualities and character traits are you passing down to your children? Are you actively involved in knowing your children, guiding them toward maturity? Or are you passively allowing their evil bents to run rampant? Remember, the legacy you leave will shape your family for generations to come.

 Living Insights STUDY ONE

In his insightful book *The Root of the Righteous*, A. W. Tozer titled one of his chapters "The Hunger of the Wilderness." In it he writes:

> Every farmer knows the hunger of the wilderness, that hunger which no modern farm machinery, no improved agricultural methods, can ever quite destroy. No matter how well prepared the soil, how well kept the fences, how carefully painted the buildings, let the owner neglect for a while his prized and valued acres and they will revert again to the wild and be swallowed up by the jungle or the wasteland. The bias of nature is toward the wilderness, never toward the fruitful field.[5]

The bias of human nature is the same. If we neglect to cultivate the fruits of the Spirit in our children, they will develop instead only a weed patch of undesirable traits (see Gal. 5:19–23).

---

4. As quoted by J. Oswald Sanders, in *A Spiritual Clinic* (Chicago, Ill.: Moody Press, 1958), p. 90.

5. A. W. Tozer, *The Root of the Righteous* (Camp Hill, Pa.: Christian Publications, 1986), p. 100.

In our previous lesson, the second Living Insight had you write out a composite sketch of your children's bents. Spend some time now considering how to nurture the good bents in each of your children.

_____

_____

_____

_____

_____

_____

_____

_____

_____

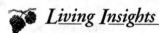 *Living Insights*

Today's lesson ended with a poignant illustration that revealed the power of legacies. Have you spent much time considering what legacies *you* will leave to your children? Have you thought about what will last the longest? What will mean the most? Probably not money or property—though both have their place. Or even family heirlooms or photo albums, as priceless as these are.

Perhaps there is nothing more precious to leave your children than memories. Memories are like pictures, living photographs that will linger on and touch your children long after you're no longer able to.

In his book *The Gift of Remembrance*, author Ken Gire reminisces on three pictures his father left him. One of those pictures, taken thirty years, twelve hundred miles, and a wife and four kids ago, was the remembrance of his father treating a mentally disabled boy with dignity and kindness. A memory that continues to shape the destiny of his own life.

I found that when I wrote my first book,
    it was about a mentally disabled boy.
When I did volunteer work,
    it was with the handicapped.
And every time I encounter those who are
    in some way bent or broken,
    my heart softens.
I send up a little prayer—
    that the load they carry
    may be made easier to bear,
    that they may be protected
    from the cruelties of this world,
    and that they may experience as much
    as they can of the goodness
    life has to offer.[6]

Aside from the material goods you plan to bequeath to your children, what memories are you giving them? Describe right now a few pictures your children will have of you in their mental scrapbooks after you're gone. Take as much time as you need to give this the thought it deserves.

6. Ken Gire, *The Gift of Remembrance* (Grand Rapids, Mich.: Zondervan Publishing House, Daybreak Books, 1990), p. 23.

Chapter 6

A CHIP OFF THE OLD BENT

Exodus 34:5–7

Physicians tell us that deformities are often hereditary, as are certain diseases and predispositions to disease. Psychiatrists state that mental illnesses and emotional problems are also sometimes inherited. It stands to reason, then, that certain spiritual characteristics may also be passed down from generation to generation.

Regarding spiritual genetics, our heritage contains three major aspects. One, every person is born in the image of God, with a God-given personality and distinct abilities (Gen. 1:26–27). Two, every person is born with a sin nature, a general bent toward evil inherited from Adam (Rom. 5:12). And three, each of us has a *specific* bent or tendency toward evil inherited from our immediate forefathers. It is this third area that we're going to investigate in our lesson today.

Evil Bent Defined and Explained

According to Scripture, everyone is born estranged from God (Ps. 51:5; 58:3; Rom. 3:10–18; Eph. 2:3; Col. 1:21).

Generally—from Adam

When Adam sinned in the Garden of Eden, he was acting as the representative of all humankind.

> Through one man sin entered into the world, and death through sin, and so death spread to all men, because all sinned. (Rom. 5:12)

We can trace the root of our evil bent back to the first man. But the fruit of that bent—the evil thoughts, words, and actions themselves—can be traced more immediately to the branches of our own family tree.

Specifically—from Mom and Dad

Think about yourself for a minute. Chances are, if you take a good look in the mirror, you'll see a striking reflection of the weaknesses you saw in your parents. The resemblance may be a violent temper, deception, sexual weakness, or anxiety. If the characteristic was a dominant gene in your parents' spiritual chemistry, you can count on its being passed down to you.

Biblical Basis for Specific Bents toward Evil

By precept and example the Bible demonstrates how specific bents toward evil branch out from each family tree.

Actual Iniquity Is Transferred

In Exodus 34:5–8, amid the clefts of Mount Sinai, Moses brushes with God's glory in an awesome daybreak encounter.

> And the Lord descended in the cloud and stood there with him as he called upon the name of the Lord. Then the Lord passed by in front of him and proclaimed, "The Lord, the Lord God, compassionate and gracious, slow to anger, and abounding in lovingkindness and truth; who keeps lovingkindness for thousands, who forgives iniquity, transgression and sin; yet He will by no means leave the guilty unpunished, visiting the iniquity of fathers on the children and on the grandchildren to the third and fourth generations." And Moses made haste to bow low toward the earth and worship.

Glinting in the morning sun, the foreboding edge of God's revelation catches our eye: "Visiting the iniquity of fathers on the children and on the grandchildren to the third and fourth generations" (v. 7b). The term *iniquity* is from a Hebrew word meaning "to bend, to twist, to distort, to pervert." In Proverbs 12:8 the term is translated "perverse."

At first glance this seems vengeful and unfair. Yet God could have allowed that same perversion or bent to continue throughout the family's history, fraying the entire family line. But God says "No—it will have rippling effects only to the third and fourth generations."[1] The scales, then, are weighted not on God's harshness

---

1. "But when, on the other hand, the hating ceases, when the children forsake their fathers' evil ways, the warmth of the divine wrath is turned into the warmth of love . . . and this mercy endures not only to the third and fourth generation, but to the thousandth generation, though only in relation to those who love God, and manifest this love by keeping His commandments." C. F. Keil and F. Delitzsch, *Commentary on the Old Testament* (Grand Rapids, Mich.: William B. Eerdmans Publishing Co., n.d.), vol. 1, pp. 117–18.

47

but on His kindness, demonstrating that He is indeed compassionate, gracious, and abounding in lovingkindness for thousands.

Families Transmit Similar Character Traits

The books of Kings and Chronicles document the civil war that split the nation of Israel into two kingdoms. The southern kingdom was ruled by Solomon's son Rehoboam. The reins to the northern kingdom, however, were given to the wicked Jeroboam, Solomon's trusted servant, who spurred the nation on to runaway sinfulness. Nineteen times in Kings we read that the nation walked in Jeroboam's sinful ways (see 1 Kings 15:34; 16:26). Those who ruled after Jeroboam inherited his sins of idolatry, immorality, and rebellion. Like three thorny vines, these bents grew out from Jeroboam and inextricably entangled themselves in the nation—until, at last, God had to brandish the pruning shears of judgment.

A Case Study: Abraham's Family

Turning back the pages of Israel's history, we'll follow a specific bent—deception—through four generations.

Abraham. Abraham's propensity to shade the truth is brought to light in Genesis 12.

> Now there was a famine in the land; so Abram went down to Egypt to sojourn there, for the famine was severe in the land. And it came about when he came near to Egypt, that he said to Sarai his wife, "See now, I know that you are a beautiful woman; and it will come about when the Egyptians see you, that they will say, 'This is his wife'; and they will kill me, but they will let you live. Please say that you are my sister so that it may go well with me because of you, and that I may live on account of you." (vv. 10–13)

The truth was that Sarah was Abraham's *half* sister. But he shaded that part of the truth. Looking further at Abraham's life, we see that this tendency to lie—a well-established bent in his character—crops up again. Look at a similar incident in Genesis 20.

> Now Abraham journeyed from there toward the land of the Negev, and settled between Kadesh and Shur; then he sojourned in Gerar. And Abraham said of Sarah his wife, "She is my sister." So Abimelech

48

king of Gerar sent and took Sarah. But God came to Abimelech in a dream of the night, and said to him, "Behold, you are a dead man because of the woman whom you have taken, for she is married." Now Abimelech had not come near her; and he said, "Lord, wilt Thou slay a nation, even though blameless? Did he not himself say to me, 'She is my sister'? And she herself said, 'He is my brother.'" . . . And Abimelech said to Abraham, "What have you encountered, that you have done this thing?" And Abraham said, "Because I thought, surely there is no fear of God in this place; and they will kill me because of my wife. Besides, she actually is my sister, the daughter of my father, but not the daughter of my mother, and she became my wife; and it came about, when God caused me to wander from my father's house, that I said to her, 'This is the kindness which you will show to me: everywhere we go, say of me, "He is my brother."'" (vv. 1–5a, 10–13)

Abraham reasoned that since Sarah was his father's daughter from another marriage, and therefore technically his half sister, he was speaking the truth. The only flaw in that line of reasoning is that he implied something entirely false—that she was *only* a sister.

Isaac. As Abraham's family tree spreads its branches, we see the seeds of this trait crop up in the second generation. The bent of lying sprouts in Isaac's life through a situation similar to the one his father had experienced years earlier.

So Isaac lived in Gerar. When the men of the place asked about his wife, he said, "She is my sister," for he was afraid to say, "my wife," thinking, "the men of the place might kill me on account of Rebekah, for she is beautiful." And it came about, when he had been there a long time, that Abimelech king of the Philistines looked out through a window, and saw, and behold, Isaac was caressing his wife Rebekah. Then Abimelech called Isaac and said, "Behold, certainly she is your wife! How then did you say, 'She is my sister'?" And Isaac said to him, "Because I said, 'Lest I die on account of her.'" And Abimelech said, "What is this you have done to us? One of the people might easily have lain with your wife, and you would have brought guilt upon us." (26:6–10)

With this same crooked bent from Abraham's life resurfacing in Isaac's life, we can't help but think, "Like father, like son."

Jacob. From there, because unchecked, this flaw was passed from Isaac to his son Jacob. Isaac and Rebekah had twin sons, Jacob and Esau, with bents that went in different directions. At an early age Jacob began to develop a Machiavellian habit of doing whatever he needed to gain the advantage, no matter how manipulative or mercenary (see 25:27–33).

Encouraged by his mother, his habit culminated in a treacherous act of deception. Jacob deceived his father Isaac into giving him the blessing that belonged to his brother. Notice how one lie was placed upon another, lending authenticity to his masquerade.

> Then Rebekah took the best garments of Esau her elder son, which were with her in the house, and put them on Jacob her younger son. And she put the skins of the kids on his hands and on the smooth part of his neck. She also gave the savory food and the bread, which she had made, to her son Jacob.
>
> Then he came to his father and said, "My father." And he said, "Here I am. Who are you, my son?" And Jacob said to his father, "I am Esau your first-born; I have done as you told me. Get up, please, sit and eat of my game, that you may bless me." And Isaac said to his son, "How is it that you have it so quickly, my son?" And he said, "Because the Lord your God caused it to happen to me." Then Isaac said to Jacob, "Please come close, that I may feel you, my son, whether you are really my son Esau or not." So Jacob came close to Isaac his father, and he felt him and said, "The voice is the voice of Jacob, but the hands are the hands of Esau." And he did not recognize him, because his hands were hairy like his brother Esau's hands; so he blessed him. And he said, "Are you really my son Esau?" And he said, "I am." So he said, "Bring it to me, and I will eat of my son's game, that I may bless you." And he brought it to him, and he ate; he also brought him wine and he drank. Then his father Isaac said to

him, "Please come close and kiss me, my son." So
he came close and kissed him; and when he smelled
the smell of his garments, he blessed him.
(27:15–27a)

So entrenched was this habit of lying that even when Jacob
was old, deception continued to persist in his life (see 43:2–6).

The Sons of Jacob

Tragically, Jacob's habit of deception became so ingrained that
it left an imprint in the lives of his sons.

Like his parents, Jacob also had his favorites, the foremost being
Joseph. But the other sons resented this. And in a jealous rage over
the interpretation of a dream Joseph had, the other brothers sold
him to a slave caravan (chap. 37). To cover the crime, they took
Joseph's distinctive, multicolored coat, dipped it in animal's blood,
and brought it to their father, explaining, "We found this; please
examine it to see whether it is your son's tunic or not" (v. 32). That
was the spoken lie. They hadn't found it. The whole scene, props
and all, was staged. The second lie was unspoken.

> Then he examined it and said, "It is my son's tunic.
> A wild beast has devoured him; Joseph has surely
> been torn to pieces!" (Gen. 37:33)

Jacob went into mourning, and his sons did not say a word. In
fact, they comforted him. By their silence, they lied. Like father,
like sons.

Some Suggestions to Sincere Yet Struggling Parents

A lesson like this can be depressing, particularly when we see
the skeletons of our own character flaws fleshed out in our children.
As genuinely concerned parents, how can we keep from passing on
those destructive bents? Here are four suggestions.

First: *Lead your child to faith in Christ.* The first and biggest step
in straightening out the bents is for your child to become aligned
with Him who is "the way, and the truth, and the life" (John 14:6).
The Holy Spirit makes that alignment possible because He works
internally to create a pliable spirit.

Second: *Ask for God's wisdom in studying your child.* Observe
your child's words (Luke 6:45) and actions (1 Tim. 5:25), because
they reflect character . . . or the lack of it.

Third: *As you set limits, be fair and consistent.* Consistency is what shapes character over the long haul. It gives your children the security they need to entrust themselves to your hands.

Fourth: *Do everything in your power to maintain open and loving communication with your child.* You will never know your child unless you take control of your schedule and plan time just to listen and observe. This may require putting the TV to bed early instead of the children. Or how about taking your child to work one day instead of bringing your work home? Whatever it takes, your child is worth it!

 Living Insights

Small children are like polished mirrors. They reflect with ingenuous clarity what they see and hear.

Timmy was like that, only more so. The mental disability that darkened his seven-year-old mind seemed to heighten his skill at mimicry. In particular, Timmy liked imitating the TV adventures he saw.

In one afternoon's outing at the zoo, he would be a policeman shooting it out with bank robbers in the gorilla house, or a gutsy soldier sneaking up on enemies in the petting zoo, or a martial arts master fighting his way through the aviary. One minute you were standing next to someone whose shoes were always on the wrong feet, and the next, he was Batman and you were Robin, battling villains in Gotham City.

Mirrors can be disquieting, however. If people cursed, Timmy cursed too. When people smoked, Timmy would find a stick and start puffing. And he knew how to throw royal temper tantrums because he'd seen others do that too. He copied it all, good and bad, as all small children do.

Mom and Dad, have you seen any of your bents toward evil suddenly staring back at you in your children's behavior or attitudes? Maybe a tendency to tell "little white lies," like Abraham, or a critical attitude or a stingy spirit? It's a little unnerving, isn't it? Let's use this time to take a close look at those flaws and what you can do to give your children something good to emulate instead. In the left column of the following chart, write down some less-than-desirable traits you have seen in yourself and now see in your children. Then, with the help of a concordance or topical Bible, list what the Bible has to say about these bents.

Family Trait	What the Bible Says

One thing remains, really, if you intend to apply what you have learned in this Living Insight: explaining it to your children. Let them see what God has to say about the crooked bents in you that they're copying. Together, confess them as sin and ask for God's help in becoming imitators of Him instead (Eph. 5:1–2).

Living Insights   STUDY TWO

Seeking cures for the problems we're facing right now is important, but it's just as important—perhaps even more important—to prevent bents toward evil from developing in the first place. In the conclusion of our lesson we gave you four over-the-counter prescriptions that can keep destructive bents from being passed on. Take a moment now to examine how effectively you're applying these prescriptions.

Preventing Bad Bents			
Four Concluding Points	Doing Great	Needs Work	Flop City
Lead your child to faith in Christ.	❏	❏	❏
Ask for God's wisdom in studying your child.	❏	❏	❏
As you set limits, be fair and consistent.	❏	❏	❏
Do everything in your power to maintain open and loving communication with your child.	❏	❏	❏

How are you doing at preventing bad bents from forming? Did you sometimes find yourself in the suburbs of "Flop City"? If so, take the time to plan a strategy for improving one of these weaker areas.

The area I'll begin working on: _____

_____

The strategy I'll be implementing: _____

_____

_____

_____

_____

_____

_____

_____

_____

_____

Chapter 7

SHAPING THE WILL WITH WISDOM

Selected Proverbs

In his excellent book *The Strong-Willed Child*, Dr. James Dobson describes the inevitable tug-of-war between the parents' will and the child's.

> It is obvious that children are aware of the con-test of wills between generations, and that is pre-cisely why the parental response is so important. When a child behaves in ways that are disrespectful or harmful to himself or others, his hidden purpose is often to verify the stability of the boundaries. This testing has much the same function as a policeman who turns doorknobs at places of business after dark. Though he tries to open doors, he hopes they are locked and secure. Likewise, a child who assaults the loving authority of his parents is greatly reassured when their leadership holds firm and confident. He finds his greatest security in a structured environ-ment where the rights of other people (and his own) are protected by definite boundaries.[1]

The objective in child rearing is not for parents to win the tug-of-war at all costs. For if you do, you may end up not only with a muddy, tearful child but also with a relationship strained beyond repair. Rather, your objective is to shape the will, gently yet firmly, as a potter would a clay vase. But that takes a special kind of wisdom—a wisdom only God can provide.

---

1. James Dobson, *The Strong-Willed Child* (Wheaton, Ill.: Tyndale House Publishers, 1978), p. 30.

Some Necessary Distinctions Worth Making

Proverbs, a veritable storehouse of godly wisdom, tells us that if we truly love our children, we'll discipline them diligently (13:24). But since the word *discipline* is so emotionally charged and so generally misunderstood, we need to make some distinctions that will help clarify the concept.

Between Abuse and Discipline

Because child abuse has reached tragic proportions today, many people avoid any kind of discipline. But there is a difference: abuse tears down a child's spirit; discipline builds it up.

Abuse is unfair, extreme, and degrading. It's unduly harsh, unnecessarily long, and totally inappropriate. When you drag children's feelings through the mud and kick them when they're down, you're being abusive. The result? A soiled self-esteem and scars that often last a lifetime. Actions like that are not discipline; they're abuse. And abuse doesn't grow out of love; it stems from hate.

Discipline is fair, fitting, and upholds the child's dignity. Discipline is built on a foundation of justice. It isn't capricious or arbitrary, so the child should have a good idea of the punishment that will be meted out if parental boundaries are willfully and defiantly violated. This form of correction strengthens rather than shatters the child's self-worth. Discipline is rooted in proper motivation—love and genuine concern—not in anger or expedience.

Between Crushing and Shaping

Proverbs 15:13 paints a vivid contrast between a spirit that has been shaped and one that has been crushed.

> A joyful heart makes a cheerful face,
> But when the heart is sad, the spirit is broken.

Proverbs 17:22 cameos a relief of a similar image.

> A joyful heart is good medicine,
> But a broken spirit dries up the bones.

The ultimate goal of discipline is to build up your children with direction and confidence, giving them a strong and secure self-esteem to carry them through life. Shaping the will nurtures a vitality for living, while crushing the will "dries up" that vitality.

Between Natural Childishness and Willful Defiance

Every child needs space in which to learn, make mistakes, and develop in the early years of growing up. As a parent, it's important for you to distinguish between childish irresponsibility and behavior that is willfully disobedient. Again, Dr. Dobson has some insightful wisdom on the subject.

> A child should not be spanked for behavior that is not willfully defiant. When he forgets to feed the dog or make his bed or take out the trash—when he leaves your tennis racket outside in the rain or loses his bicycle—remember that these behaviors are typical of childhood. It is, more than likely, the mechanism by which an immature mind is protected from adult anxieties and pressures. Be gentle as you teach him to do better. If he fails to respond to your patient instruction, it then becomes appropriate to administer some well-defined consequences (he may have to work to pay for the item he abused or be deprived of its use, etc.). However, childish irresponsibility is very different from willful defiance, and should be handled more patiently.[2]

Several Suggestions Worth Considering

Shaping the will with wisdom is a critical task of parenting. Here are some suggestions that should make it easier and more effective.

Start Early

We look again to Proverbs for wisdom to carry out this awesome responsibility. In 13:24 Solomon provides some practical hints.

> He who spares his rod hates his son,
> But he who loves him disciplines him diligently.

The word *diligently* has a colorful background in the Hebrew. Originally, it meant "dawn" or "early morning." Later it evolved into the idea of pursuing something early in life—like a career—and thus came to mean "with determination" or "with diligence." The

2. Dobson, *The Strong-Willed Child*, p. 32.

association of *diligence* with discipline indicates that we should start disciplining our children early in their lives. The longer we wait to begin the process, the more difficult it will become (compare 19:18).

Stay Balanced

Balance is what keeps children from falling off their bicycles and skinning their knees. Balance also keeps parents from crashing when it comes to discipline. Two kinds of discipline are mentioned in the Bible. Both complement each other, but both must be kept in balance.

First, let's look at *physical discipline*. Proverbs 22:15 describes this category of discipline.

> Foolishness is bound up in the heart of a child;
> The rod of discipline will remove it far from him.

The rod indicates the infliction of pain. Once again we turn to Dr. Dobson as he underscores the importance of the child being able to associate wrongdoing with pain.

> If your child has ever bumped his arm against a hot stove, you can bet he'll never deliberately do that again. He does not become a more violent person because the stove burnt him; in fact, he learned a valuable lesson from the pain. Similarly, when he falls out of his high chair or smashes his finger in the door or is bitten by a grumpy dog, he learns about physical dangers in his world. These bumps and bruises throughout childhood are nature's way of teaching him what to fear. They do not damage his self-esteem. They do not make him vicious. They merely acquaint him with reality. In like manner, an appropriate spanking from a loving parent provides the same service. It tells him there are not only physical dangers to be avoided, but he must steer clear of some social traps as well (selfishness, defiance, dishonesty, unprovoked aggression, etc.).[3]

The second kind of discipline is *verbal discipline*. This category of correction, also known as reproof, is found in Proverbs 3:11–12.

---

3. James Dobson, *Hide or Seek*, rev. ed. (Old Tappan, N.J.: Fleming H. Revell Co., 1979), p. 95.

My son, do not reject the discipline of the Lord,
Or loathe His reproof,
For whom the Lord loves He reproves,
Even as a father, the son in whom he delights.

Reproof is not a tongue-lashing with cutting remarks that lacerate character. It is verbal instruction arising out of a genuine and deep-felt delight in the child (note the word *delights* in verse 12). Proverbs 29:15 shows verbal reproof in balance with physical discipline: "The rod and reproof give wisdom."

Be Consistent

When you're under pressure, it's easy to let expediency determine how and when you discipline your child—a case of the urgent squeezing out the important. But the rule shouldn't be expediency; it should be consistency. Here are a few guidelines to ensure that your discipline will be consistent.

1. Make sure the rules are known beforehand.
2. Discipline privately.
3. Explain the violation and its consequences.
4. Administer the rod soundly.
5. Tenderly hold your child after the spanking.
6. Assure your child of your love and concern.

Be Reasonable

As a child grows older, there comes a time when it is inappropriate to use the rod. If you're not sensitive to this, you will end up demeaning rather than disciplining your child.

Significant Goals Worth Implementing

You may miss the mark on discipline from time to time, but if you don't have a goal in sight, you're likely to miss every time you try. To stay on target, here are a couple of goals to aim at.

For Yourself

Model God's role of authority until your child reaches the point where there is a natural transfer of that authority from you to God.

For Your Children

Help them cultivate a healthy respect for themselves and others so they can be strong enough and secure enough to stand up under the pressures of life.

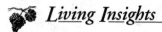

While growing up, many of us came to associate the word *discipline* with only one thing—*punishment*, usually of the dreaded "wait till your father gets home" kind.

But as Bruce Ray explains in his book *Withhold Not Correction*, discipline is more than simply punishment.

> Biblical discipline is *correction*, and that means that the pattern of the child's behavior must be *changed by instruction* in righteousness. He must be shown the error of his way, and then directed to the proper path. This requires explanation and instruction. Biblical discipline demands words.[4]

Too many parents rely on punishment alone to discipline their children. But by doing that, they're neglecting to give their kids the assistance they need in understanding and applying God's Word to their lives.

How well-prepared are you to shape your children's wills with the wisdom of God's Word? Are you training them in the way they should go or punishing them for going in the way they shouldn't?

The book of Proverbs is loaded with nuggets of wisdom to help train in righteousness—discipline—your children. With the help of a concordance, dig through Proverbs for words like *discipline*, *child*, *rod*, and any others you think might be valuable. In the space provided keep a record of your findings.

Key Word   Wisdom from Proverbs

_____   _____

                   _____

_____   _____

                   _____

_____   _____

                   _____

---

4. Bruce A. Ray, *Withhold Not Correction* (Phillipsburg, N.J.: Presbyterian and Reformed Publishing Co., 1978), p. 87.

_____   _____

_____   _____

_____   _____

_____   _____

_____   _____

_____   _____

_____   _____

                         _____

In addition to your study of Proverbs, here's a chart[5] you might find helpful in bringing your children up in the Lord. Use it as a primer for further study on your own.

God's Will for Our Attitudes		
_Is_ . . .	_Not_ . . .	_Key Passages_
Love	Lust	Romans 14:13–19 1 Corinthians 13:1–13 Romans 13:14
Reliance	[Willfulness]	Proverbs 3:5–6 Galatians 5:16
Humility	Pride	James 4:6 Philippians 2:5–8
Gratitude	Presumption	Colossians 3:17
Clear Conscience	Guilt	Romans 14:22–23
Integrity	Irresponsibility	Colossians 3:17, 22
Diligence	Laziness	Colossians 3:23
Eagerness	Compulsion	1 Peter 5:2
Generosity	Selfishness	1 Timothy 6:17–19
Submission	Self-advancement	1 Peter 5:5–6
Courage	Cowardice	John 16:33 Matthew 10:26–28
Contentment	Greed	Hebrews 13:5 Philippians 4:11

5. Garry Friesen, _Decision Making and the Will of God_ (Portland, Oreg.: Multnomah Press, 1980), p. 156.

A fascinating link often exists between how you were disciplined as a child and how you discipline your children. Using the four suggestions made in this study, reflect on how your parents disciplined you.

Were they diligent about starting early? When?

_____

_____

Did they balance the physical and verbal aspects of your discipline? How?

_____

_____

Was the discipline consistent in your home? Explain.

_____

_____

How reasonable do you think your parents were? Why?

_____

_____

If you have children at home, write out how you can use the suggestions from our study to wisely discipline them. Note especially the areas you feel need to be changed from the way you were brought up.

_____

_____

_____

_____

For further study, read *Dare to Discipline* by James Dobson, *The Key to Your Child's Heart* by Gary Smalley, or *How to Really Love Your Child* by Ross Campbell.

Chapter 8

ENHANCING ESTEEM

Ephesians 5:25–29; Selected Proverbs

O ne of the greatest contributions family members can make to one another is to enhance each person's self-esteem. Odds are, if it doesn't happen at home, it probably won't happen at all. Unfortunately, family members are often better at putting each other down than building each other up. They use their words as swords rather than scalpels, to hurt rather than heal.

> There is one who speaks rashly like the thrusts of
>   a sword,
> But the tongue of the wise brings healing.
> (Prov. 12:18)

Contrary to the childhood chant "Sticks and stones may break my bones, but words will never hurt me," cutting words do hurt. They penetrate deeply into a person's heart, slashing self-esteem to ribbons.

In today's lesson, rather than explore ways to eviscerate esteem, we'll examine some ways to enhance it.

Essential Value of Self-Esteem

Ephesians 5:25–30 focuses on the marriage relationship, but its principle is universal.

> Husbands, love your wives, just as Christ also loved the church and gave Himself up for her; that He might sanctify her, having cleansed her by the wash-ing of water with the word, that He might present to Himself the church in all her glory, having no spot or wrinkle or any such thing; but that she should be holy and blameless. So husbands ought also to love their own wives as their own bodies. (vv. 25–28a)

The universal principle we can derive from this is: The love we show our spouses, or anyone else, ought to be in direct proportion to the love we have for ourselves. And this love for ourselves is not a noisy conceit, but a quiet sense of self-worth.

Components of Its Development

From Paul's marital insights in verses 28b–30 we can call two important actions to enhance the development of self-esteem in our children.

> He who loves his own wife loves himself; for no one ever hated his own flesh, but nourishes and cherishes it, just as Christ also does the church, because we are members of His body.

The first component is found in the word *nourish*. The Greek word is *ektrephō*. Its root, *trephō*, can mean "to bring," and the prefix *ek* means "out." It is most often used in a context relating to children, as in Ephesians 6:4, and has the idea of feeding, caring for, and drawing out the child. The word implies that there are things deep within the child which parents should draw out.

The second component is revealed in the word *cherish*. The Greek word here is *thalpō*, meaning "to heat or keep warm." It pictures tenderness, holding someone close to keep them warm. In the Greek translation of the Hebrew Old Testament, called the Septuagint, it is used of a bird sitting on her eggs (Deut. 22:6). In the New Testament it is used of the tenderness of a nursing mother (1 Thess. 2:7).

Putting the two components of nourishing and cherishing together conveys the distinct impression that enhancing your child's self-esteem requires a great amount of attention and affection. Within every child are certain God-given characteristics. As those characteristics are "drawn out" and "warmed," the self-esteem of that child begins to grow stronger.

Compensations for Its Absence

When self-esteem is lacking, people often put up defenses—covering up, rationalizing, or aggressively asserting themselves. They may also wear masks—a plastic smile or a constant frown—to hide their hurt or insecurity. It's been said: Scratch a humorist and you'll find a sad man. Humor often becomes a mask for a hurting person to hide behind. Ask any comedian. Onstage humor stems from offstage hurt, a truth Proverbs 14:13 corroborates—"Even in laughter the heart may be in pain."

Culmination of Its Presence

When your children have strong self-esteem, they are free to be everything God created them to be. They can accept and love others because they have first accepted and loved themselves. And they will have a calm sense of security and a deep sense of satisfaction independent of performance or peer recognition.

Are you committed to giving your children the invaluable gift of a strong sense of self-worth? If so, it will be reflected in your words. Words like, "Nice job, Son" or "Thanks, Honey. That was so thoughtful of you."

Are those the words that greet your children when they come home from school? Or do the words "How many times have I told you . . . " or "Do it right or don't do it at all" cut into their tender hearts?

Remember, life and death are in the power of the tongue—the life of your child's self-esteem, or its death.

Biblical Insights on Cultivating Self-Esteem

Returning to Ephesians 5, we can construct both a theological basis and a philosophical framework for cultivating self-esteem.

Theological Basis

Verses 28–29 suggest two crucial points. First, a good self-esteem is God's desire for us because it provides the foundation to love others. And second, God sees worth and value in each of us, for we are nourished and cherished by Christ.

Philosophical Framework

Verses 25–30 answer the question, Why should we love ourselves?

> Husbands, love your wives, just as Christ also loved
> the church and gave Himself up for her. (v. 25)

Loving ourselves enables us to unselfishly love others. It also allows us to bring out the best in others, as Christ does with us,

> that He might present to Himself the church in all
> her glory, having no spot or wrinkle or any such thing;
> but that she should be holy and blameless. (v. 27)

Finally, it helps us to be more like Christ Himself.

> For no one ever hated his own flesh, but nourishes
> and cherishes it, just as Christ also does the church,
> because we are members of His body. (vv. 29–30)

65

Practical Suggestions

From the wealth of Proverbs come three gems of wisdom, parental qualities your children will treasure forever.

First: *A commitment to discover.* Deep within the heart are concealed the secrets of one's life, caved away like a subterranean spring. Parents, therefore, must be committed to digging down deep and drawing out that sparkling water hidden in their children.

> A plan in the heart of a man is like deep water,
> But a man of understanding draws it out.
> (Prov. 20:5)

Second: *A willingness to get involved.* As a file hones the edges of a knife, so a sharpening of the soul occurs when two people intimately and intensely interact.

> Iron sharpens iron,
> So one man sharpens another. (27:17)

If your family wants to sharpen each other emotionally, you have to get involved emotionally. If you want to sharpen each other spiritually, you must get involved spiritually. If you want to sharpen each other mentally, you have to get involved mentally. You need to be there for your children, actively helping them grow.

Third: *An ability to reflect.* Just as we need mirrors around the house to see if our hair is in place, so we need family members to reflect our inner self in order for us to see what's going on inside. In that reflection is where our identity comes into focus.

> As in water face reflects face,
> So the heart of man reflects man. (27:19)

Children also see just how much they are valued in our eyes. And as water reflects best when calm and still, so do we.

Personal Ways to Encourage Self-Esteem

By now, you may be asking *how*. How do I, as a parent, discover my child? How do I get involved? How do I reflect? Here are two ways to help do those things and thus encourage your child's self-worth.

Develop Good, Open Communication

Good communication is not churchy little homilies complete with organ accompaniment; but real talk for the real world. Not pious words from the pulpit; but transparent teaching from your own life.

Help Each Child Compensate

Find areas of strength in your children's lives, and help them develop these to compensate for weaker areas. If a child isn't athletic, for example, focus on artistic or musical development. Help your children discover their unique, God-given abilities and talents.

A Concluding Thought

Roy Croft, in his poem "Love," shows how love cherishes and nourishes . . . how it discovers, gets involved, and reflects . . . how it draws out and develops the loved one's self-esteem.

> I love you,
> Not only for what you are,
> But for what I am
> When I am with you.
>
> I love you,
> Not only for what
> You have made of yourself,
> But for what
> You are making of me.
>
> I love you,
> For the part of me
> That you bring out;
> I love you
> For putting your hand
> Into my heaped-up heart
> And passing over
> All the foolish, weak things
> That you can't help
> Dimly seeing there,
> And for drawing out
> Into the light
> All the beautiful belongings
> That no one else had looked
> Quite far enough to find.
>
> I love you because you
> Are helping me to make

Of the lumber of my life
Not a tavern
But a temple;
Out of the works
Of my every day
Not a reproach
But a song.[1]

 Living Insights

In *The Sensation of Being Somebody*, author Maurice Wagner writes that the three essentials of healthy self-esteem are *belongingness*, feeling accepted and wanted by others; *worthiness*, having a sense of value; and *competence*, feeling adequate to carry out life's daily situations. "These three feelings," Wagner explains, "blend together in the formation of self-concept like three tones of a musical chord. At times each can be considered separately, but usually it is impossible to distinguish one from the other."[2]

The harmonious tones of a healthy self-esteem can be disrupted, however, by the discordant notes of hostility, guilt, and fear.

> Hostility contradicts feelings of belongingness; guilt cancels feelings of worthiness. Hostility says, in effect, "You are bad, I don't like you." Guilt says, "I am bad, you could not like me. I loathe myself." . . .
>
> Fear tends to paralyze the mind and cause it to function inadequately. Fear and its close associate, anxiety, cancel the "I can" feelings of competence so that a person is inclined to think "I can't" about many things.[3]

Just as a sensitive conductor can detect a flat note while listening to a full orchestra, so, too, sensitive parents can detect a flat note of self-esteem in their families by listening to the prevailing tone of the family.

1. Roy Croft, as quoted in *The Best Loved Poems of the American People*, selected by Hazel Felleman (Garden City, N.Y.: Doubleday and Co., 1936), p. 25.

2. Maurice Wagner, *The Sensation of Being Somebody* (Grand Rapids, Mich.: Zondervan Publishing House, 1975), p. 32.

3. Wagner, *Sensation of Being Somebody*, pp. 44–45.

Play back in your mind the family conversations you participated in or heard over the last couple of days. Now do this again, only this time erase the actual words and simply listen to the family tone and what's being communicated by it. Do the conversations in your home resonate with belongingness, worthiness, and competence? Or is there a cacophony of hostility, guilt, and fear? Use the space provided to identify what's being communicated and to whom.

_____

_____

_____

Is there a flat note in the self-esteem of one of your children? Which of the three tones—belongingness, worthiness, or competence—needs tuning?

_____

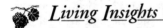 *Living Insights*   STUDY TWO

Today a variety of equations for building your child's self-esteem are on the market. Trouble is, though, none of them balance.

> One such equation is *Appearance + Admiration = a Whole Person.* This equation does not balance because we are not the sum and total of how we appear or what others admiringly think of us.
>
> Another such equation which does not balance is *Performance + Accomplishments = a Whole Person.* We are more than the sum total of our skills and the recognized abilities we have developed.
>
> A third equation might be *Status + Recognition = a Whole Person.* This equation is also untrue, for we are more than anyone thinks of us.[4]

None of these equations satisfy our needs for belongingness, worthiness, and competence with any lasting effect. Appearance, performance, and status are all pawns of circumstance. None of them come with any guarantees.

4. Wagner, *Sensation of Being Somebody*, p. 162.

The only equation that truly balances is *God + Me = a Whole Person*. And this is guaranteed. Let's listen to Maurice Wagner.

> The meaning of the equation of self-identity, *God + Me = a Whole Person*, is this: My belongingness is secured and reaffirmed by my love for God my Father and validated by His love for me. My worthiness is secured and reaffirmed by my love for Jesus Christ His Son and validated by His love for me. My competence is secured and reaffirmed in daily situations of life through the ministry and love of the Holy Spirit as He uses the Word of God to instruct, correct, and reassure me; my competence is validated as I live by the Word of God.[5]

Looking back, can you identify which equation you were raised to believe?

Which are you teaching your children today? (Hint: Consider which equation is reflected most in your lifestyle and attitudes.)

Do you want to enhance your children's self-esteem? Then commit to helping them *discover* the spiritual equation for a healthy self-esteem. Get *involved* in teaching them the eternal biblical truths the equation rests upon. And last, *reflect* these truths in your relationships with your children.

For further study, use a concordance or your Bible and cross-reference the following verses.

Belongingness	Worthiness	Competence
Rom. 8:15–17	Ps. 139:15–16	John 14:26; 16:7–15
Gal. 3:26–29; 4:4–7	Matt. 6:24–30	2 Cor. 12:9–10
Eph. 1:5–6	Rom. 8:32–39	Phil. 4:13

Also, read *The Sensation of Being Somebody* by Maurice Wagner.

---

5. Wagner, *Sensation of Being Somebody*, p. 167.

Chapter 9

CHALLENGING YEARS
OF ADOLESCENCE
(PART ONE)
Judges 11:1–8; 2 Samuel 13–16

Adolescence. Could there be a more difficult time in life? Hormones race through your body like horses out of a starting gate. A huge pimple erupts on your nose the day of The Big Date. Your voice cracks to broadcast that you're still not a man yet.

This time of transition closes the door on childhood. Baseball cards give way to driver's licenses. Dolls give way to boyfriends. Dressup gives way to proms. Lazy vacation days give way to summer jobs.

Childhood is behind you, forever locked away. And there you stand on the threshold of adult life, biting your nails. Your knees are knocking, and it seems the entire world is watching as you take that uncertain first step. All the while, your body is giving you a shove. And with a thud you stumble unceremoniously into adulthood.

Some Significant Questions Adolescents Ask

During this slippery time, it is no wonder adolescents begin exchanging exclamation points for question marks. In groping to find their balance and stand on their own two feet, they question even the very ground that supports them. The questions are legion, but they generally fall into four main categories.

Who Am I?

This first question emerges out of the struggle adolescents have with *identity*. As everything begins to change in a teenager's life, the question "Who is the real me?" becomes central.

What Attitudes Will I Choose?

Prior to adolescence a child learns to be submissive to Mom and Dad. But as the child begins to grow up, the question of *responsibility* is raised. In childhood, the consequences of irresponsible behavior were buffered. Adulthood, however, has a way of exacting consequences from the irresponsible decisions we make. Adolescents want the right to be independent, but they struggle with accepting the attendant responsibilities.

Whose Role Will I Respect?

This question involves the struggle over *authority*. As adolescents try to discover where they fit into society, they also begin to question the pillars of authority undergirding that society. Authority figures are everywhere: parents, teachers, principals, coaches, policemen, employers. "Whom do I follow? How far? And for how long?" Questions like these peck away at a teenager's thinking.

What Will Be My Lifestyle?

During childhood most children adopt their parents' values. If their parents avoid alcohol, they do too. If their parents go to church, they go along. If their parents value education, so do they. But when adolescence emerges, everything is up for grabs. The struggle becomes one of *conformity*. They ask themselves, "Which road will my life take? The way of my parents? My peers? The public? Will I be a follower and adopt someone else's lifestyle, or will I chart a path of my own?"

The Struggles of Two Adolescents in the Bible

To demonstrate that the struggles of adolescence aren't confined to those in our generation, let's go back in time to examine two other adolescents, Jephthah and Absalom. As we take a look at some incidents in their adolescent days, we'll see how their responses helped shape their adult life.

Jephthah

Judges 11 introduces Jephthah to us.

> Now Jephthah the Gileadite was a valiant warrior, but he was the son of a harlot. And Gilead was the father of Jephthah. And Gilead's wife bore him sons; and when his wife's sons grew up, they drove Jephthah out and said to him, "You shall not have an inheritance in our father's house, for you are the son of another woman." So Jephthah fled from his brothers and lived in the land of Tob; and worthless fellows gathered themselves about Jephthah, and they went out with him. (vv. 1–3)

Unwanted and rejected, Jephthah struggled with identity. Cut out of the will and kicked out of the home, he no doubt asked himself, "Who am I?" For an answer he turned to his friends, a gang of good-for-nothings, the type that Proverbs warns against in 1:10–19. And while he's hanging out with these hoods, he's on a quiet but desperate search for himself.

Before we go further with Jephthah's story, let's consider an important issue revealed in his life—the influence of friends. Proverbs 13:20 speaks directly to this matter:

> He who walks with wise men will be wise,
> But the companion of fools will suffer harm.

Jephthah fell into the companionship of fools—"worthless fellows," says Scripture. How about your children? Do you know who your kids' companions are? Have you ever talked with them about the qualities of a good friend? Are you equipping them to make good decisions regarding their choice of friends? You should be, if you want to help them grow wisely into adulthood. For the shape of your children's future is molded largely by those who surround them, which will most likely be their peers rather than their parents.

As we turn back to Jephthah's life, we find that, even as an adult, he still searched for identity and needed acceptance. That's what made the offer to be leader over all who lived in Gilead so appealing (Judg. 11:9), despite his deep feelings of resentment.

> And it came about after a while that the sons of Ammon fought against Israel. And it happened when the sons of Ammon fought against Israel that the elders of Gilead went to get Jephthah from the land of Tob; and they said to Jephthah, "Come and be our chief that we may fight against the sons of Ammon." Then Jephthah said to the elders of Gilead, "Did you not hate me and drive me from my father's house? So why have you come to me now when you are in trouble?" And the elders of Gilead said to Jephthah, "For this reason we have now returned to you, that you may go with us and fight with the sons of Ammon and become head over all the inhabitants of Gilead." So Jephthah said to the elders of Gilead, "If you take me back to fight against the sons of Ammon and the Lord gives them up to me, will I

become your head?" And the elders of Gilead said to Jephthah, "The Lord is witness between us; surely we will do as you have said." Then Jephthah went with the elders of Gilead, and the people made him head and chief over them; and Jephthah spoke all his words before the Lord at Mizpah. (vv. 4–11)

Absalom

After the rape of his sister by their half-brother Amnon and the passive response of his father, Absalom was left with a jigsaw of puzzling attitudes to fit together. One thing he puzzled over was responsibility—"What attitude should I choose?" For two years resentment stirred in Absalom's heart toward his father David. And for two years hatred toward Amnon simmered, until it turned into a rolling boil. At last, that seething cauldron of resentment and hatred spilled over into an act of vengeance.

> And Absalom commanded his servants, saying, "See now, when Amnon's heart is merry with wine, and when I say to you, 'Strike Amnon,' then put him to death. Do not fear; have not I myself commanded you? Be courageous and be valiant." (2 Sam. 13:28)

As it was commanded, so it was done (v. 29). And after the murder, Absalom fled

> and went to Talmai the son of Ammihud, the king of Geshur. And David mourned for his son every day. (v. 37)

To whom did he run? To Talmai, his maternal grandfather (2 Sam. 3:3). And for what was he looking? Roots, security, direction. For three years Absalom stayed with Talmai (13:38). Then, after some persuasion from Joab, David had Absalom brought back to Jerusalem . . . but something was wrong.

> The king said, "Let him turn to his own house, and let him not see my face." So Absalom turned to his own house and did not see the king's face. (14:24)

After a three-year absence, you would think Absalom and David would have wanted to see each other, talk things out, make things right. But a wall of resentment stood between them. For two years Absalom lived in Jerusalem, and for two years that wall remained

74

(v. 28). As Absalom grew from adolescence to adulthood, he attempted to hurdle that wall in an effort to see his father and remove the bitter stones that stood between them.

> Then Absalom sent for Joab, to send him to the king, but he would not come to him. So he sent again a second time, but he would not come. Therefore he said to his servants, "See, Joab's field is next to mine, and he has barley there; go and set it on fire." So Absalom's servants set the field on fire. Then Joab arose, came to Absalom at his house and said to him, "Why have your servants set my field on fire?" And Absalom answered Joab, "Behold, I sent for you, saying, 'Come here, that I may send you to the king, to say, "Why have I come from Geshur? It would be better for me still to be there."' Now therefore, let me see the king's face; and if there is iniquity in me, let him put me to death." (vv. 29–32)

So Joab agreed to take Absalom's request to the king.

> When Joab came to the king and told him, he called for Absalom. Thus he came to the king and prostrated himself on his face to the ground before the king, and the king kissed Absalom. (v. 33)

But seeing his father didn't tear down the wall between them. Nothing was revealed of their talking things out or making things right—only a kiss. And even that was nondescript and apparently without feeling. This perfunctory kiss pushed Absalom over the edge and set him on a collision course with his father.

> Now it came about after this that Absalom provided for himself a chariot and horses, and fifty men as runners before him. And Absalom used to rise early and stand beside the way to the gate; and it happened that when any man had a suit to come to the king for judgment, Absalom would call to him and say, "From what city are you?" And he would say, "Your servant is from one of the tribes of Israel." Then Absalom would say to him, "See, your claims are good and right, but no man listens to you on the part of the king." Moreover, Absalom would say,

"Oh that one would appoint me judge in the land, then every man who has any suit or cause could come to me, and I would give him justice." And it happened that when a man came near to prostrate himself before him, he would put out his hand and take hold of him and kiss him. And in this manner Absalom dealt with all Israel who came to the king for judgment; so Absalom stole away the hearts of the men of Israel. (15:1–6)

With those stolen hearts, Absalom forged an insurrection.

But Absalom sent spies throughout all the tribes of Israel, saying, "As soon as you hear the sound of the trumpet, then you shall say, 'Absalom is king in Hebron.'" Then two hundred men went with Absalom from Jerusalem, who were invited and went innocently, and they did not know anything. And Absalom sent for Ahithophel the Gilonite, David's counselor, from his city Giloh, while he was offering the sacrifices. And the conspiracy was strong, for the people increased continually with Absalom. (vv. 10–12)

And if conspiracy weren't enough of a dagger to thrust in his father's heart, Absalom twisted the blade with a personal affront.

Then Absalom said to Ahithophel, "Give your advice. What shall we do?" And Ahithophel said to Absalom, "Go in to your father's concubines, whom he has left to keep the house; then all Israel will hear that you have made yourself odious to your father. The hands of all who are with you will also be strengthened." So they pitched a tent for Absalom on the roof, and Absalom went in to his father's concubines in the sight of all Israel. (16:20–22)

Earlier, Absalom chose the attitudes of resentment, rebellion, and retaliation. Later, he refused to repent. Finally, he openly revolted against his father's authority.

Insights for Parents to Ponder

The stories of Jephthah and Absalom leave behind at least two striking insights for parents today.

First: *Few things are more damaging to an adolescent than rejection.* Jephthah is a case in point. It's hard enough to struggle with identity and self-esteem at this age, but feeling rejected makes those difficult times virtually impossible. As a parent, try to be especially affirming during your child's adolescent years. And try not to condemn. Remember, "the tongue of the wise brings healing" (Prov. 12:18b).

Second: *Few things are more essential to an adolescent than communication.* This was what Absalom wanted so desperately from his father—but he never got it. One opportunity after another slipped through David's fingers. Until it was too late . . . and he saw his son slip away forever.

 ## Living Insights STUDY ONE

During adolescence, when teens are caught in a tug-of-war between adulthood and childhood, they have an intense need to feel accepted. And if this need isn't met at home, they'll search till it is met elsewhere—just as Jephthah did. He found a rabble of mercenaries to associate with who were every parent's worst nightmare. But he didn't care. At least they accepted him for who he was, and that was all that mattered.

Unlike Jephthah's situation, however, the reason many teens feel rejected at home is because they've never been taught the difference between acceptance and approval. Author David Seamands writes,

> When a child is being punished for something not approved by his parents, it is easy for him to get the idea that they don't like him or accept him as a person. Thus a kind of mathematical formula is implanted in the youngster:
>
> Approval means acceptance.
>
> Disapproval means nonacceptance or rejection.
>
> So punishment and discipline equals disapproval and rejection. . . .
>
> This may or may not be the parents' fault. However, if you are a parent it would be well to look closely at just how you discipline your children. Be

> sure to make it crystal clear that while you do not
> approve of what they are doing, you do accept and
> love them as your children. . . . Make clear to
> them that your acceptance of them does not depend
> on your approval of everything they do.[1]

Mom and Dad, have you communicated to your children that your love for them is not based on how well they perform? This week, what can you do to make the distinction between acceptance and approval crystal clear to your children?

_____

_____

_____

_____

_____

To help make your child's journey through adolescence a little less bumpy, listen to James Dobson's cassette tape series titled "Preparing for Adolescence," which is published by One Way Library, and read Rich Buhler's insightful book *Love: No Strings Attached* (Nashville, Tenn.: Thomas Nelson Publishers, 1987).

 Living Insights

> "Give careful heed to my words,
> and let that be the comfort you offer me."
> (Job 21:2 REB)

"Parents don't listen." It's a familiar complaint among teens. And you know what? They're right.

Now, before you—

"What do you mean I don't listen? Boy, can you believe this guy?"

What I meant was—

---

1. David Seamands, *Putting Away Childish Things* (Wheaton, Ill.: Scripture Press Publications, Victor Books, 1982), pp. 90–91.

"I know what you meant, and you're WRONG. Have you ever tried having a rational conversation with a teenager? They're the ones who don't listen!"

You're right. Teenagers don't listen either. In fact, nobody does.

"Huh?"

You see, nobody is born a listener. Sure, we have ears to hear things with, but that's not the same as listening. Listening is a skill that has to be developed like any other. The problem, of course, is that few people are willing to expend the energy it takes to progress beyond being rookie hearers to becoming skilled listeners.

Norman Wright, in his book *Communication: Key to Your Marriage*, writes:

> Listening is more than politely waiting for your turn to speak. It is more than hearing words. Real listening is receiving and accepting the message as it is sent—seeking to understand what the other person really means.[2]

Did you catch the word *understand*? If your goal in communication is to understand the other person, then you're well on your way to being a skilled listener and to improving your chances at keeping the communication lines open between you and your teens.

If, however, your goal in communication is to dominate, to control, to win, then you're not listening, not really. People who approach communication with this attitude typically hear only what they want to hear, they concentrate more on what they want to say than on what the other person is saying, and they tend to interrupt others before they're finished.[3] Three surefire methods for disconnecting all lines of meaningful communication between two people.

Now if you want to stay close to your teens and help them move closer to the Lord throughout adolescence, start listening with the goal of understanding.

Here's a simple test to help you get started. Though it's from Norm Wright's book on marriage, it still applies—just write in your child's name in the spaces provided.

---

2. H. Norman Wright, *Communication: Key to Your Marriage* (Glendale, Calif.: Gospel Light Publications, Regal Books, 1974), p. 55.

3. For a look at what the Bible has to say about people like this, see Proverbs 18:13 and 29:20 and James 1:19–20.

How would you describe yourself as a listener? . . .

When _____ talks, do you go beyond the facts being discussed and try to sense how he or she is feeling about the matter?

        Yes   No   Sometimes

Do certain things or phrases _____ says prejudice you so that you cannot objectively listen to what is being said?

        Yes   No   Sometimes

When you are puzzled or annoyed by what _____ says, do you try to get the question straightened out as soon as possible?

        Yes   No   Sometimes

. . . .

When you are listening to _____ are you easily distracted by outside sights and sounds (such as the TV set)?

        Yes   No   Sometimes[4]

Can you find any clues in your answers for improving your listening skills?

_____

_____

_____

_____

For further help on communication skills, we wholeheartedly recommend the following: Os Guinness' excellent chapter on listening, titled "A Time to Listen," in his book *In Two Minds*; Norm Wright's book *Communication: Key to Your Marriage*; and *How to Talk So Your Teenager Will Listen* by Paul Swets.

---

4. Wright, *Communication: Key to Your Marriage*, pp. 56–57.

Chapter 10

CHALLENGING YEARS OF ADOLESCENCE
(PART TWO)
2 Chronicles 34:1–27; Daniel 1:3–21

Jim Conway's book Men in Mid-Life Crisis refers to the period of midlife as a "second adolescence." In developing that idea, Conway points out four major enemies of a man in the throes of that crisis.

Enemy number one: his body. He is losing his hair, losing his looks, and losing his physique. Odds are, the only thing he isn't losing is weight.

Enemy number two: his work. The thrill of his job is quietly being replaced by monotony. He often asks himself: "How in the world did I ever get stuck in a job like this?"

Enemy number three: his wife and family. His responsibilities at home make him feel trapped. Even though he wants to find a more fulfilling career, he can't leave his job and forget about his family's needs.

Enemy number four: his God. The man in midlife pictures God leaning over the pulpit of heaven, pointing an accusatory finger, and preaching incriminations at him: "You're selfish, you're lazy, and you're filled with lust." In response, the man lashes back and blames God for giving him his frail body, along with its drives and weaknesses.

Yes, second adolescence is not a bad label for those going through a midlife crisis. And it tells us a lot about how adolescents feel as well. Similar to midlife men, they, too, have four major enemies: identity, responsibility, authority, and conformity. We covered the first two in the previous lesson. Now we'll examine the last two.

Two Questions—Two Teens

Teenagers wrestle with a number of questions as they go through the traumatic transition of adolescence. Two of those questions concern authority and conformity. And two teenagers whose lives lived out right answers to those questions were Josiah and Daniel.

Josiah

Josiah's grandfather, King Manasseh, ruled Judah for fifty-five years. During most of that time he led the people away from God. Following on the heels of Manasseh came Josiah's father, Amon. The final verses of 2 Chronicles 33 document both his morally destitute character and his mutinied demise.

> Amon was twenty-two years old when he became king, and he reigned two years in Jerusalem. And he did evil in the sight of the Lord as Manasseh his father had done, and Amon sacrificed to all the carved images which his father Manasseh had made, and he served them. Moreover, he did not humble himself before the Lord as his father Manasseh had done, but Amon multiplied guilt. Finally his servants conspired against him and put him to death in his own house. (vv. 21–24)

To fill the throne, the people looked to eight-year-old Josiah. Remarkably, considering his family tree, Josiah developed an unswerving obedience to God (34:2). Instead of throwing off the yoke of the Lord, as his father and grandfather had done, Josiah chose to follow the role model of another predecessor.

> For in the eighth year of his reign while he was still a youth, he began to seek the God of his father David. (v. 3a)

The Hebrew word for *seek* is *darash*. It means "to seek with care, to inquire, to search out." At the age of sixteen, Josiah made a serious, diligent search to know God. As a result, he made a conscious decision that the Lord would be his authority and he would listen to His counsel. And first and foremost on the list God gave Josiah was the command to purify the country by eliminating idolatry.

> And in the twelfth year he began to purge Judah and Jerusalem of the high places, the Asherim, the carved images, and the molten images. And they tore down the altars of the Baals in his presence, and the incense altars that were high above them he chopped down; also the Asherim, the carved images, and the molten images he broke in pieces and ground to powder and scattered it on the graves of

those who had sacrificed to them. (vv. 3b–4)

At twenty, fresh out of adolescence, Josiah stood up and put an end to two generations of wickedness. What was it that molded him to take a stand like that? Whatever it was in Josiah, we know it didn't come from his father. Second Kings 22:1 provides a clue.

> Josiah was eight years old when he became king, and he reigned thirty-one years in Jerusalem; and his mother's name was Jedidah the daughter of Adaiah of Bozkath.

Usually, the new ruler's father is listed in these biblical accounts of the kings. But here we see Josiah's mother. Why? Probably because she was the primary influence in his life. In 2 Chronicles 34 we pick up Josiah at twenty-six and see an incredible heart for the things of God—a heart his mother probably helped cultivate.

> Now in the eighteenth year of his reign, when he had purged the land and the house, he sent Shaphan the son of Azaliah, and Maaseiah an official of the city, and Joah the son of Joahaz the recorder, to repair the house of the Lord his God. And they came to Hilkiah the high priest and delivered the money that was brought into the house of God, which the Levites, the doorkeepers, had collected from Manasseh and Ephraim, and from all the remnant of Israel, and from all Judah and Benjamin and the inhabitants of Jerusalem. . . .
>
> When they were bringing out the money which had been brought into the house of the Lord, Hilkiah the priest found the book of the law of the Lord given by Moses. And Hilkiah responded and said to Shaphan the scribe, "I have found the book of the law in the house of the Lord." And Hilkiah gave the book to Shaphan. . . . Shaphan the scribe told the king saying, "Hilkiah the priest gave me a book." And Shaphan read from it in the presence of the king. And it came about when the king heard the words of the law that he tore his clothes. Then the king commanded Hilkiah, Ahikam the son of Shaphan, Abdon the son of Micah, Shaphan the scribe, and Asaiah the king's servant, saying, "Go, inquire of

the Lord for me and for those who are left in Israel and in Judah, concerning the words of the book which has been found; for great is the wrath of the Lord which is poured out on us because our fathers have not observed the word of the Lord, to do according to all that is written in this book." (vv. 8–9, 14–15, 18–21)

Parents—don't underestimate the influence of your son or daughter. If Josiah could change a nation, your child can change the course of a peer group, or even an entire school.

Daniel

As a young man, Daniel struggled successfully with the question of conformity. Most of us remember Daniel from the lions' den. But we forget that the steel-tempered courage of Daniel's later life was forged on the anvil of his adolescence. For it was during Daniel's adolescence that he and his Jewish compatriots were taken captive to Babylon by Nebuchadnezzar.

> Then the king ordered Ashpenaz, the chief of his officials, to bring in some of the sons of Israel, including some of the royal family and of the nobles, youths in whom was no defect, who were good-looking, showing intelligence in every branch of wisdom, endowed with understanding, and discerning knowledge, and who had ability for serving in the king's court; and he ordered him to teach them the literature and language of the Chaldeans. (Dan. 1:3–4)

What is Nebuchadnezzar trying to do? Mold them into good Babylonian citizens. These monotheistic, straight-laced Jewish boys have been brought to the big city, with its enormous pressure to conform. And then they're given a crash course in Babylonian life.

> And the king appointed for them a daily ration from the king's choice food and from the wine which he drank, and appointed that they should be educated three years, at the end of which they were to enter the king's personal service. (v. 5)

So great was the pressure to conform that they were even given new names—Babylonian names (vv. 6–7). But Daniel was determined not to let his external label affect his inner commitment to God.

Daniel made up his mind that he would not defile himself with the king's choice food or with the wine which he drank. (v. 8a)

So Daniel proposed a test.

He sought permission from the commander of the officials that he might not defile himself. Now God granted Daniel favor and compassion in the sight of the commander of the officials, and the commander of the officials said to Daniel, "I am afraid of my lord the king, who has appointed your food and your drink; for why should he see your faces looking more haggard than the youths who are your own age? Then you would make me forfeit my head to the king." But Daniel said to the overseer whom the commander of the officials had appointed over Daniel, Hananiah, Mishael and Azariah, "Please test your servants for ten days, and let us be given some vegetables to eat and water to drink. Then let our appearance be observed in your presence, and the appearance of the youths who are eating the king's choice food; and deal with your servants according to what you see." (vv. 8b–13)

With some skepticism, no doubt, the overseer agreed to a ten-day trial run.

And at the end of ten days their appearance seemed better and they were fatter than all the youths who had been eating the king's choice food. So the overseer continued to withhold their choice food and the wine they were to drink, and kept giving them vegetables. (vv. 15–16)

Finishing the king's course of study, Daniel graduated valedictorian, with his three friends following right behind him.

And as for these four youths, God gave them knowledge and intelligence in every branch of literature and wisdom; Daniel even understood all kinds of visions and dreams. Then at the end of the days which the king had specified for presenting them, the commander of the officials presented them before Nebuchadnezzar. And the king talked with them, and out of them all not one was found like Daniel, Hananiah, Mishael and Azariah; so they entered the king's personal service. And as for every matter of wisdom and understanding about which the king consulted them, he found them ten times better than all the magicians and conjurers who were in all his realm. (vv. 17–20)

The secret to Daniel's unique favor with the Lord? He made up his mind that he wouldn't defile himself. And he followed through with that commitment.

Two Practical Lessons

These two remarkable teenagers—Josiah and Daniel—wrestled and triumphed over the questions of authority and conformity. From them we can learn two practical lessons.

First: *Adolescents must be given room to make up their minds.* You've got to give them room—even if that means they fail. Your counsel is valuable. Your support is valuable. Your influence is valuable. But taking your hand away and letting them walk on their own two feet is also valuable. And you must do that if they are ever to learn to walk.

Second: *Personal convictions stand the test better than forced convictions.* From dieting to doctrinal statements, adults know the reality of this lesson. When you decide something based on your deep inner convictions, you will better handle any temptations and trials than if those convictions were forced on you. The same is true for teenagers. Share your convictions, but don't be dictatorial. Patiently allow your teenagers to explore and develop their own convictions.

Living Insights STUDY ONE

In his excellent book *The Screwtape Letters*, C. S. Lewis wrote about the process God uses to raise His children.

> He wants them to learn to walk and must therefore take away His hand; and if only the will to walk is really there He is pleased even with their stumbles.[1]

---

1. C. S. Lewis, *The Screwtape Letters* (New York, N.Y.: Macmillan Publishing Co., 1961), p. 39.

One lesson we learned in our study is that adolescents must be given room to make up their own minds. When you give them room and take away your hand, they are more vulnerable to a fall. But remember, it is in falling that they develop a stable walk. Be there to pick them up and dust them off, but don't hold their hand through all the tough decisions in life. Give them room. Give them a chance to think on their own.

Is there some area of your children's lives in which you still try to take them by the hand? Think through the following areas and see what you can do to help your children think more independently in each one.

Money _____

_____

_____

_____

Music _____

_____

_____

_____

Clothes _____

_____

_____

_____

Church _____

_____

_____

_____

Friends _____

_____

_____

_____

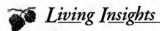 *Living Insights*

We've come far enough in our study to merit a breather. Let's pause to review—an excellent way to underscore what we've learned. Let's review our learning from Scripture. Next to each lesson title, write the biblical truth that touched you most in that particular lesson, and summarize one way you applied it.

I. Laying the Foundation

1. An Endangered Species? _____

_____

_____

_____

2. Masculine Model of Leadership _____

_____

_____

_____

3. Positive Partner of Support _____

_____

_____

_____

4. Your Baby Has the Bents (Part One) _____

_____

_____

_____

5. Your Baby Has the Bents (Part Two) _____

_____

_____

_____

6. A Chip off the Old Bent _____

_____

_____

_____

II. Building the Structure

7. Shaping the Will with Wisdom _____

_____

_____

_____

8. Enhancing Esteem _____

_____

_____

_____

9. Challenging Years of Adolescence (Part One) _____

_____

_____

_____

10. Challenging Years of Adolescence (Part Two) _____

_____

_____

_____

Chapter 11

WARNING THE UNINVOLVED
1 Samuel 1–4

The deterioration of a house, once teeming with life, is a tragic thing to see. Rafters sagging like slumped shoulders under the burden of decades. Ceilings mapped with remembered rain from shingles too weary to withstand the elements. Windows, once bursting with morning light, now silted over from neglect. A pall of somber, gray dust shrouding its derelict interior.

There are no voices in the old house. No lively talk over the dinner table. No laughter. Only an infrequent, musty wheeze from the attic . . . an occasional arthritic creak in the ceiling joists . . . a nostalgic sigh for memories past.

It's a sad sight.

But even more sad, more tragic, is the slow disintegration of a family. In this lesson, we'll witness one such family. And, hopefully, the signs of deterioration will stand out so glaringly as to motivate us to make the necessary repairs before our homes suffer a similar fate.

Meet the Family

Turning back the yellowed pages of time, we come to an ancient account of a disintegrating family in 1 Samuel 1–4. Unfortunately, we see no pictures of the mother propped on this family's mantle. Instead, our eyes are drawn to a portrait of the father's relationship with his two natural sons and one adopted son.

The Father: Eli

Next to the large center portrait sit three small pictures framing separate aspects of Eli's life—professional, personal, and physical—

pictures that form a composite of this pillar in Israel's community. Like many respected men today, Eli was called upon to assume a position of leadership in the community. First and foremost was his role as high priest (1:9b). Besides his ceremonial role, Eli served in a civil capacity as a judge—a position he occupied for forty years (4:18).[1] Added to these professional responsibilities, Eli also had the personal responsibility of being a father to two sons (1:3).

As we view the third picture, we discover several physical qualities about Eli. In chapter 2, verse 22, we see that he "was very old." And attendant with that was failing vision (3:2b).[2] In 4:18 two more facts about Eli become visible—one negative, one positive.

> And it came about when [the messenger] mentioned the ark of God that Eli fell off the seat backward beside the gate, and his neck was broken and he died, for he was old and heavy. Thus he judged Israel forty years.

The man was severely overweight, a fact that contributed to his death. But, as a legacy, he left behind a forty-year record of faithful service—at least in regard to his professional life. He didn't fare so well, however, in his parental responsibilities.

The Two Natural Sons: Hophni and Phinehas

Professionally, Eli's sons followed in their father's footsteps as priests (1:3b). Morally, however, they took a different path.

> Now the sons of Eli were worthless men; they did not know the Lord. (2:12)

The remainder of chapter 2 chronicles their cavalier attitude toward sin and their cynicism toward their spiritual duties. Not only did they not know the Lord, but they disregarded the priestly customs (vv. 13–17). And their personal lives, as well as their hearts, were far from God. So much so that they sinned blatantly by lying with "the women who served at the doorway of the tent of meeting"

---

1. The tone of the passage and Eli's comments confirm his faith in God. In fact, his name literally means "Jehovah is high" or, more likely, "Jehovah-my God" (meaning, "Jehovah is my God").

2. Eli eventually went blind by age ninety-eight (1 Sam. 4:15). But despite the decline of his physical eyesight, his spiritual eyes were as sensitive as ever. When God was speaking to Samuel, Eli sensed it was the Lord and wisely instructed the young boy how to respond (3:8–9).

(v. 22b). Catching a gust of this gossip circulating among the people, Eli confronted his sons.

> And he said to them, "Why do you do such things,
> the evil things that I hear from all these people? No,
> my sons; for the report is not good which I hear the
> Lord's people circulating. If one man sins against
> another, God will mediate for him; but if a man
> sins against the Lord, who can intercede for him?"
> (vv. 23–25a)

Their response, however, revealed hearts that were stubborn and rebellious.

> But they would not listen to the voice of their father,
> for the Lord desired to put them to death. (v. 25b)

Over in the New Testament, the apostle Paul's words in Ephesians 4:18–19 describe Hophni and Phinehas to a tee.

> Being darkened in their understanding, excluded
> from the life of God, because of the ignorance that
> is in them, because of the hardness of their heart;
> and they, having become callous, have given them-
> selves over to sensuality, for the practice of every
> kind of impurity with greediness.

When a person's heart resists spiritual truth, then that truth is external to the person. So every rub that person has with spiritual things does not spark a fire within the heart but forms a callus on the surface instead.

That's what every brush with their priestly responsibilities did to Hophni and Phinehas. They resisted truth, resented authority, and finally rebelled openly.

The same thing often happens with preachers' kids or any children continually exposed to churchy talk, churchy meetings, and churchy people. Some go through the motions like marionettes on a string. They walk. They talk. They bend at the joints. They look real, but inside is a heart of wood. Some even become cynical and cut away the restricting strings.

We who are parents must ask ourselves: Are we making our children into wooden puppets who dance on strings, or are we helping them become real people who delight in spiritual things? Are we lighting fires within their hearts, or rubbing calluses on the surface?

The Adopted Son: Samuel

Born to Hannah and Elkanah as a special gift from God, Samuel was given over to the Lord's service in grateful response to His blessing (see 1 Sam. 1). Growing up in Eli's home, Samuel was raised by a foster father who was passive, aging, overweight, and rapidly losing touch with his children. On top of that, he had to share the home with two rebellious, older brothers.

Like a fragrant flower planted in a garbage dump, Samuel stood in stark contrast to the moral stench of Hophni and Phinehas. Yet, in this considerably less than ideal soil, young Samuel flourished, serving the Lord (2:11) and developing into a strong young man.

> Thus Samuel grew and the Lord was with him
> and let none of his words fail. (3:19)

This verse reveals that God protected and nurtured the tender spirit of Samuel. In the same way, He can watch over the lives of our children too.

Their home may be full of weeds. Their school may be rocky soil. The moral climate around them may be tempestuous.

God, however, is a remarkable gardener. And if we dedicate our children to the Lord, no matter what garbage dump they're on, He can put a greenhouse of grace around them—and make something fruitful of their lives.

Observe the Activity

If we had lived down the street from Eli's house, we would have had a pretty good idea of what went on there just by casting a glance in that direction.

Sins of the Sons

So shamelessly sinful were Hophni and Phinehas that they engaged in flagrant immorality at the very doorway of the tent of meeting (2:22). And "all Israel" was aware of it. So repugnant was their rebellion and so wishy-washy was their father's response that God finally stepped in with an irreversible judgment.

> "For I have told him that I am about to judge his house forever for the iniquity which he knew, because his sons brought a curse on themselves and he did not rebuke them." (3:13)

Warnings of Others

If you read through the account, you will find several categories of messengers the Lord used to warn of His impending intervention. The first warning was in the form of a public report.

> "The report is not good which I hear the Lord's people circulating." (2:24)

The second warning came from an unnamed prophet.

> Then a man of God came to Eli and said to him, ". . . the Lord God of Israel declares, 'I did indeed say that your house and the house of your father should walk before Me forever'; but now the Lord declares, 'Far be it from Me—for those who honor Me I will honor, and those who despise Me will be lightly esteemed. Behold, the days are coming when I will break your strength and the strength of your father's house so that there will not be an old man in your house. And you will see the distress of My dwelling, in spite of all that I do good for Israel; and an old man will not be in your house forever. Yet I will not cut off every man of yours from My altar that your eyes may fail from weeping and your soul grieve, and all the increase of your house will die in the prime of life. And this will be the sign to you which shall come concerning your two sons, Hophni and Phinehas: on the same day both of them shall die.'" (vv. 27a, 30–34)

The final warning was from God Himself in the form of a vision to young Samuel.

> And the Lord said to Samuel, "Behold, I am about to do a thing in Israel at which both ears of everyone who hears it will tingle. In that day I will carry out against Eli all that I have spoken concerning his house, from beginning to end." (3:11–12)

And Samuel, in turn, conveyed the prophecy to Eli (vv. 15–18).

Response of the Father

Eli's way of dealing with his shameful sons was equivalent to a verbal slap on the hand—and a mild one at that.

And he said to them, "Why do you do such things, the evil things that I hear from all these people? No, my sons; for the report is not good which I hear the Lord's people circulating." (1 Sam. 2:23–24)

Eli was not only incomplete in his reproof, he even indulged his sons, as God's rebuke to him indicates.

"Why do you kick at My sacrifice and at My offering which I have commanded in My dwelling, and honor your sons above Me, by making yourselves fat with the choicest of every offering of My people Israel?" (v. 29)

By not intervening when they took such huge portions of meat for themselves, Eli was indulging his sons' sin. A final thing we note about Eli's response is a sort of passive fatalism.[3] Note how he resigns himself when he hears Samuel's prophecy.

"It is the Lord; let Him do what seems good to Him." (3:18b)

Signs of Domestic Disintegration

OK, we've met the family and observed the activity in and around the home. Now it's time to do a little evaluating. If we look closely, we will find at least four corrosive agents that helped erode Eli's family.

First: *Preoccupation with his profession to the exclusion of his family's needs.* Eli's intense focus on his responsibilities as priest and judge relegated his family to a blur in the background. No wonder he missed the faults in their formative years; they were never in focus in the first place. Alexander Whyte remarks:

Let me consider well how, conceivably, it could come about that Hophni and Phinehas could be born and brought up at Shiloh and not know the Lord? Well, for one thing, their father was never at home. What with judging all Israel, and what with sacrificing and interceding for all Israel, Eli never saw his children

3. Had Eli been obedient to the Law of Moses in the first place, he would have taken action that would have prevented his sons from bringing such shame upon the family, the priesthood, and the nation (see Deut. 21:18–21).

till they were in their beds. 'What mean ye by this ordinance?' all the other children in Israel asked at [sic] their fathers as they came up to the temple. And all the way up and all the way down again those fathers took their inquiring children by the hand and told them all about Abraham, and Isaac, and Jacob, and Joseph, and Moses, and Aaron, and the exodus, and the wilderness, and the conquest, and the yearly passover. Hophni and Phinehas were the only children in all Israel who saw the temple every day and paid no attention to it.[4]

Second: *Refusal to face the seriousness of his sons' lifestyle.* When the reports of his sons' sin sharpened his focus, Eli refused to realize the gravity of the report. He must have ached inside—such a success at work and such a failure at home. Yet he rationalized away both the causes and the far-reaching consequences of his sons' actions. Now his sons serve as examples to be avoided rather than emulated—trenchant illustrations of Proverbs 19:18.

Discipline your son in his early years while there is hope. If you don't you will ruin his life. (LB)

Third: *Failure to respond correctly to the warnings of others.* God has ways of making the blind see—even parents who are blind to their children's faults. Sometimes His ways are miraculous; often, however, they are mundane. For He can use a teacher or a neighbor or a policeman. And yes, even a grandparent. How receptive are you when these people issue their warnings? How respectful? How appreciative? Do you listen, or do you get defensive? Remember the proverb,

Where there is no guidance, the people fall,
But in abundance of counselors there is victory.
(11:14)

Fourth: *Condoning the wrong, thereby becoming a part of the problem.* Take a closer look at a verse we saw earlier and see the Lord's stinging indictment.

"Why do you kick at My sacrifice and at My offering which I have commanded in My dwelling, and honor

4. Alexander Whyte, *Bible Characters* (London, England: Oliphants, 1952), vol. 1, pp. 218–19.

your sons above Me, by making *yourselves* fat with
the choicest of every offering of My people Israel?"
(1 Sam. 2:29, emphasis added)

Did you notice that *yourselves* is plural? Some of Eli's own weight
came from adopting his sons' ways. He went from passive indiffer-
ence to active indulgence. Centuries later the prophet Jeremiah,
walking through the ruins of Jerusalem, lamented how sins are
passed from one generation to another.

Our fathers sinned, and are no more;
It is we who have borne their iniquities. (Lam. 5:7)

Such is the recycled reality of sin. Yesterday's lunch, today's
litter; and tomorrow's garbage will all stack up—on the family's
front porch.

Living Insights

In *Traits of a Healthy Family,* author Dolores Curran points out
that Americans traditionally judge families as "good" or "bad" based
on exterior signs like affluence, church attendance, and community
involvement. Accordingly, "A good family

> . . . was one that was self-sufficient, didn't ask for
> help from others, supported its institutions, was
> never tainted with failure, starved before it went on
> welfare, and met all the criteria of good families as
> determined by community and church.
>
> People paid little attention to what went on
> *inside* a family—whether there was good communi-
> cation, emotional support, or trusting relationships.
> People were only concerned about whether a family
> met the more obvious, visible family standards set
> by society.[5]

Eli was the head of a "good family." He held the top position
in his field for forty years. You could imagine him as president of the
Kiwanis Club in Ephraim or chairman of several prestigious boards
in Shiloh. Yes sir, Eli's professional reputation was impeccable.

5. Dolores Curran, *Traits of a Healthy Family* (Minneapolis, Minn.: Winston Press, 1983), p. 7.

But then there was his parental reputation. The character of his two sons, Hophni and Phinehas, didn't exactly turn out to be impeccable. Poor Eli. Were he alive today, some would probably shake their heads and say, "I just don't understand why those two ne'er-do-well boys aren't like their father. He's such a good priest and hard worker." Success at work, however, doesn't necessarily guarantee success at home. Curran writes:

> We know that families aren't good simply because of these characteristics. Yes, on the outside, a family can be successful in an American sense of the word. Its members can be achievers and possess lots of property. They can be church-goers, with the parents' marriage intact. Sadly, the family members can be miserable inside that family.[6]

Is your family a "good family"? Do you take as many pains in your parental responsibilities as you do in your professional duties? Take a moment to evaluate the health of your home in the light of Eli's mistakes.

Are you preoccupied with your profession to the exclusion of your family's needs?

❑ blindly so   ❑ partially so   ❑ not at all

Are you refusing to face serious problems in your children's life-styles?

❑ wearing blinders ❑ passively peeking ❑ eyes wide open

Do you respond correctly to the warnings of others?

❑ turn a deaf ear   ❑ hear but ignore   ❑ hear and heed

Do you become part of the problem by condoning the wrongs your children commit?

❑ partner in crime   ❑ mildly disapprove ❑ act firm in love

What happened to Eli can happen to any of us. God has recorded his mistake as a danger signal for us today. Is God warning *you* about a certain area of your family life that needs correction?

---

6. Curran, *Traits of a Healthy Family*, p. 13.

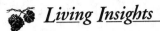

Hophni and Phinehas might gladly have traded the privileges that came with having a high priest and judge for a father for just one experience similar to what occurred to a teen named John.

> "The best time I have had with my dad was when burglars broke into our summer cottage at the lake. The police said we should come up to see what was missing. Well, our whole family's made the trip dozens of times, but this time there were just the two of us. It's a six hour drive. I'd never spent six hours alone with him in my whole life. Six hours up, six hours back. No car radio. We really talked. It's like we discovered each other. There's more to him than I thought. It made us friends." [7]

Did Hophni or Phinehas ever have six hours alone with Eli? One hour? Thirty minutes? Was Eli ever more than just Israel's high priest to them? Was he ever their father, their friend? If the way Hophni and Phinehas behaved is any indication, it seems that the three lived separate lives under the same roof.

When was the last time you really talked—alone and uninterrupted—with one of your children?

_____

_____

In what ways have you shared yourself with a family member rather than just sharing an activity?

_____

_____

In what ways have you developed closeness with your children? Have you spent as much time and energy with them as with your friends?

_____

_____

7. Curran, *Traits of a Healthy Family*, p. 42.

What would you share about your faith if you had your child's company for six uninterrupted hours?

_____

_____

_____

Many good books are available today that deal with the topic of communication. Two that might be helpful to you are *The Power of Modeling* by Jorie Kincaid and *How to Really Love Your Child* by Ross Campbell, M.D.

 ## Digging Deeper

The acid test of whether people are qualified to lead is not a seminary degree . . . not how many books they have published . . . not how spellbinding their sermons are . . . not the sophistication of their social skills.

If not these, then what?

The true test of their ability to lead others is their report card from home. In fact, 1 Timothy 3:4–5 lists this as an absolute essential of a leader:

> He must be one who manages his own household well, keeping his children under control with all dignity (but if a man does not know how to manage his own household, how will he take care of the church of God?).

What, then, does this say about Eli?

The contrast between Eli's leadership in the nation and in his own home is disturbing, bringing some unsettling questions to the surface: Does his failure at home tarnish or even negate the success of his ministry? Should he have been removed as priest of God's house until he had put his own house in order? In light of the condition of his family, was Eli even qualified to lead the people of Israel?

Allowing his sons to grow untended like noxious weeds certainly did give the tendrils of failure a foothold in Eli's ministry. Yes, he served for forty years, but look at the quality and end result of his service. The people's holy offerings were defiled (1 Sam. 2:12–17); the people themselves were degraded (v. 22); Eli's sons were exalted above the Lord (v. 29); the ark of the covenant, one of the nation's most sacred possessions, was captured by an ungodly enemy (5:11–22); and even Eli's descendants were later entangled in the mass of unwieldy growth that was his life (2:30–33).

Eli's leadership of Israel was greatly marred by his lack of leadership at home. But though this is true, it does not mean that we should cast Eli's example aside as worthless.

Probably the most important thing we can take from his story is a more solid understanding of God's requirements for leadership given in 1 Timothy. It's as if God points us to Eli and says, "This is why it is so important to follow My commands. I don't want My church, My body, to go through what Eli once put Israel through." Our world is in desperate need of true leaders. Aspiring to fill this role is commendable but at the same time sobering, because leadership is a lifestyle, not just a forty-hour-per-week job. Before we appoint leaders or seek a leadership position ourselves, let's remember Eli and look first at the home. Because that's where true leadership begins.

If you would like to do some further exploring on this issue of leadership, we would like to recommend the following books.

Covey, Stephen R. *The Seven Habits of Highly Effective People: Restoring the Character Ethic.* New York, N.Y.: Simon and Schuster, 1989. This is a secular work that can be valuable when read with a biblical perspective. The main theme is to return to the character values that are developed from within.

Sanders, J. Oswald. *Spiritual Leadership.* Revised edition. Chicago, Ill.: Moody Press, 1980. This is the classic Christian treatment of what it means to be a leader. It is standard reading for many pastors.

Swindoll, Charles R. *Leadership: Influence That Inspires.* Waco, Tex.: Word Books, 1985. This easy-to-read book gives a concise description of a leader according to biblical principles.

Chapter 12

WHEN BROTHERS AND SISTERS BATTLE

Selected Scriptures

In his book *The Strong-Willed Child*, Dr. James Dobson comments on the scourge of sibling rivalry:

> If American women were asked to indicate the most irritating feature of child rearing, I'm convinced that sibling rivalry would get their unanimous vote. Little children (and older ones too) are not content just to hate each other in private. They attack one another like miniature warriors, mobilizing their troops and probing for a weakness in the defensive line. They argue, hit, kick, scream, grab toys, taunt, tattle, and sabotage the opposing forces.[1]

If your home is a war zone of sibling rivalry and you often find yourself in a foxhole waving a little white flag, this lesson could deploy the reinforcements you need to survive the battle.

Sibling Rivalry: The Biblical Record

The earliest record of a family feud is in the fourth chapter of Genesis, a grisly reminder of the aftereffects of the Fall (vv. 1–8). Before the Fall, the first man and woman bore God's likeness.

> This is the book of the generations of Adam. In the day when God created man, He made him *in the likeness of God.* (5:1, emphasis added)

But after the Fall, that pristine image was defaced. From then on, the image was no longer exclusively God's, but also man's; it would bear the craggy features of sin.

> When Adam had lived one hundred and thirty years, he became the father of a son in *his own likeness,*

---

1. James Dobson, *The Strong-Willed Child* (Wheaton, Ill.: Tyndale House Publishers, 1978), p. 126.

according to his image, and named him Seth. (v. 3, emphasis added)

Several Examples

As we forage our way through Genesis, we can easily glean from its fertile chapters several examples of sibling rivalry.

Cain and Abel. By the time Adam's boys reached maturity, sibling rivalry was already deeply rooted—one garden Adam obviously tended with a negligent hand. In fact, the rivalry became so severe that it came to a bloody resolution the day Cain killed his brother in a field (4:8–15).[2]

Jacob and Esau. In the home of Isaac and Rebekah, parental loyalties were divided right down the middle. Isaac pulled at Esau; Rebekah tugged at Jacob. And it eventually tore the family apart (25:28). Although Esau was the rightful heir to the lion's share of his father's estate, his mother's favoritism led her to conspire with Jacob to deceive the patriarch into conferring his blessing upon Jacob rather than Esau (27:1–27). This fanned the coals of Esau's anger, which had been smoldering for years over unresolved conflict with his brother (v. 36). In his burning rage, he plotted to kill Jacob when their father died (v. 41).

Jacob's sons. Joseph was the favored son in Jacob's family. All the brothers knew it—and resented it. So severe was this war of sibling rivalry that they plotted to kill Joseph (37:18). But given a cool moment to reconsider, his hotheaded brothers sold Joseph into slavery instead, quenching the embers of hate that glowed in their hearts (v. 28).

Three Observations

In each of the stories we've studied, hatred blazed so intensely that murderous thoughts inflamed hearts and singed consciences. Three observations emerge from what we've seen thus far. One, *no family is immune to sibling rivalry.* The homes we've looked into are some of the most prominent in the Old Testament. Two, *no family problem is unique.* Sibling rivalry weaves a stubborn thread through the centuries. And three, *no solution is easy.*

A Special Case Study: David's Family

David. A man after God's own heart. Giant-killer. King.

---

2. The Hebrew in verse 8 literally says that Cain *slit the throat* of his brother.

Songwriter. Warrior. He was idolized by generations . . . but, as we will see, this idol had feet of clay. For although he was successful on the throne, he was a failure at home.

General Atmosphere of the Home

David ascended to the throne when he was thirty years old and reigned for forty years (2 Sam. 5:4–5). No longer was he an obscure shepherd boy. He was now the single most important person in Israel. No longer was he surrounded by obstinate sheep, but by obsequious servants who responded to his slightest wish. No longer did he spend the night on the hard ground under the stars, but in the plush splendor of the palace.

Times had changed. And so had David. The king had become preoccupied with the throne. From breakfast until bedtime he was faced with one decision after another. He became obsessed. And one of those obsessions involved women, which 2 Samuel 5:13 makes note of.

> Meanwhile David took more concubines and wives
> from Jerusalem, after he came from Hebron; and
> more sons and daughters were born to David.

In all, David had at least eight wives, which resulted in twenty sons and a daughter.[3] Add his concubines to that number, and you have the full-blown cast for a prime-time soap opera. Think of the jealousy that must have existed between the wives and concubines—not to mention between the children. Whatever problems you have at home, David had them compounded with interest! Hardly the home in which to raise healthy, happy children.

Specific Conflicts between the Children

As time passed and the children of this tangled family grew, you can imagine the knotty circumstances that came up and the frayed feelings that resulted from family feuds (see chaps. 13–18).[4]

A brother disgraces his sister. Second Samuel 13:1–14 records the shameful rape of Tamar by Amnon, her half brother.

---

3. The number twenty includes David and Bathsheba's son who died as a result of God's judgment of their adultery (2 Sam. 12:9–19). Besides children borne by his wives, David also fathered children by his many concubines, although none are specifically named in the Scriptures (2 Sam. 5:13; 1 Chron. 3:9).

4. These tragic conflicts within David's family grew out of the sordid soil of his past: his affair with Bathsheba and the murder of her husband Uriah (2 Sam. 11).

He took hold of her and said to her, "Come, lie with me, my sister." But she answered him, "No, my brother, do not violate me, for such a thing is not done in Israel; do not do this disgraceful thing! . . . " However, he would not listen to her; since he was stronger than she, he violated her and lay with her. (vv. 11b–12, 14)

Hatred festers between half brothers. Even though Tamar's loyal brother Absalom urged her to sweep the scandal under the rug, he couldn't sweep it from his heart.

But Absalom did not speak to Amnon either good or bad; for Absalom hated Amnon because he had violated his sister Tamar. (v. 22)

Absalom murders Amnon. In the absence of a father who would deal with the crisis, hostility simmered in the pressure cooker of Absalom's heart until at last it spewed forth in an act of vengeance.

And Absalom commanded his servants, saying, "See now, when Amnon's heart is merry with wine, and when I say to you, 'Strike Amnon,' then put him to death. Do not fear; have not I myself commanded you? Be courageous and be valiant." (v. 28)

Absalom becomes a rebellious runaway. David was so busy with his job that he was remiss in his family responsibilities. But finally the problems at home got so out of hand that they intruded upon his professional life.

After Absalom murdered his brother, he knew that his father would at last have to step in and deal with the situation. So he fled (vv. 34–39). But the story doesn't stop there. Absalom rallied support to lead a conspiracy against his father in an attempt to wrest the reins of power from David's hands (chaps. 15–17). But the coup failed, and Absalom was killed (chap. 18, especially vv. 9–15). Upon hearing of Absalom's death, David was pierced to the heart with grief—grief not only over Absalom's death, but about his failure as a father.

And the king was deeply moved and went up to the chamber over the gate and wept. And thus he said as he walked, "O my son Absalom, my son, my son

Absalom! Would I had died instead of you, O Absalom, my son, my son!" (v. 33)

Principles for Today

Through his negligence as a father, David had sown the wind only to later reap the whirlwind. But as the dust settles around the controversies that circled his throne, a few principles for today become clear—principles that can guide our homes.

Fight Passivity

The pressures of professional and personal life are so demanding that it's easy to neglect the really important things in life—like raising our families. If families are going to hold together, parents have to roll up their sleeves and get involved. No one can be an effective parent *in absentia*. And no one can parent by proxy, delegating the responsibility to someone else.

Communicate Clearly

Make sure you clearly communicate to your children where the fence lines are—those boundaries for your children's protection—and delineate the consequences of climbing over those fences. And when you're setting those fence posts for your children, be sure to sink them in the concrete of fairness and justice, so they stand straight and true.

Discipline Firmly

Once a child has crept past a fence that you've established for your home, consistent consequences must follow. Rules lose their effectiveness if they are not enforced. In turn, children lose a sense of security when they realize the fences don't mean anything.

Maintain Authority

Like Absalom, your children will often try to usurp your authority and, in some cases, overthrow it. But when you give in, it may very well result in anarchy. As long as you treat children fairly, they won't threaten your right to rule.

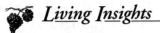

Remember these?

"That's mine!"
"I had it first."
"Did not."
"Did too."
"Give it back, booger face!"

Christie yells, "Mommm! Jimmy called me a booger face," then whispers, "You little worm, you're in trouble now."

Realizing his peril, Jimmy takes a deep, plaintive breath and wails, "Mommma, Christie's being mean and calling me names and . . ."

Christie tries to shush Jimmy with a shove.

Jimmy counters with a hard whack to Christie's shin and a no-holds-barred bedroom brawl of pinching, punching, and hair pulling ensues.

Finally, Mom comes in and . . .

Think back for just a moment. How would *your* parents have handled this?

_____

_____

_____

Some parents respond to sibling quarrels like this with a detached, "I'm busy, you work it out." Others tend to threaten both parties with something worse than death if they don't "leave each other alone and be quiet!" Then there are those who habitually blame the oldest without even bothering to look up from what they're doing.

What about your parents? Did they foster a Christlike reconciliation of fairness and forgiveness between you and your siblings? Or were you left to fight for your own rights, keeping your anger and hurt stuffed down so as not to disturb the "family peace"? In his book *The Strong-Willed Child,* James Dobson emphasizes that establishing an equitable system of justice in the home is an important parental responsibility.

There should be reasonable "laws" which are enforced

fairly for each member of the family. For purposes of illustration, let me list the boundaries and rules which have evolved through the years in my own home.

1. Neither child is *ever* allowed to make fun of the other in a destructive way. Period! This is an inflexible rule with no exceptions.

2. Each child's room is his private territory. There are locks on both doors, and permission to enter is a revokable privilege. (Families with more than one child in each bedroom can allocate available living space for each youngster.)

3. The older child is not permitted to tease the younger child.

4. The younger child is forbidden to harass the older child.

5. The children are not required to play with each other when they prefer to be alone or with other friends.

6. We mediate any genuine conflict as quickly as possible, being careful to show impartiality and extreme fairness.[5]

If you look closely, you'll find all four of our lesson's concluding principles at work in Dobson's six rules. He and his wife are actively involved, communicating clearly, disciplining firmly, and maintaining authority.

Are there equitable rules to govern the sibling rivalry in *your* home? In the space provided, write down how you typically respond. Then, after that, evaluate your response in light of the four principles from our study. Do any new rules need to be adopted?

Typical response: _____

_____

_____

_____

_____

_____

5. James Dobson, *The Strong-Willed Child* (Wheaton, Ill.: Tyndale House Publishers, 1978), p. 132.

Evaluation: _____

_____

_____

_____

_____

_____

New rules: _____

_____

_____

_____

_____

_____

🍇 *Li__ving Insights*

After a study like this, our thoughts are naturally drawn to our own brothers and sisters. If we're honest, most of us have to admit that we had our share of sibling rivalry. If you could go back in time and relive those relationships, what would you change?

_____

_____

_____

_____

_____

_____

_____

_____

_____

_____

_____

What would you change in your children's relationships with each other so that they will be able to look back years from now with pleasant, rather than painful memories of their siblings?

_____

_____

_____

_____

_____

_____

_____

_____

_____

Chapter 13

CONFRONTING THE UNPLEASANT

Luke 15:11–24

The pain of having a prodigal child. Can any pain be more disorienting for a parent? More defeating? More devastating? What do you do when a child is too stubborn to listen? Too angry to reason with? Too old to spank?

John White, in his excellent book *Parents in Pain*, provides a biblical answer.

> God's dealings with his people form a pattern for Christian parents. Like him we may eventually have to allow our persistently rebellious children to harvest the consequences of their willfulness. The time can come when we have to withdraw all support from them and oblige them, because of their own decisions, to leave home.[1]

Hard words. But as we will see in today's study, they are wise words.

God's Response to a Rebellious Will

In the Old Testament era, God took a bold, uncompromising stand on rebellion.

An Indictment from the Old Testament

Rebellious children were as much a problem in ancient times as they are today. The method of dealing with the problem back then, however, was considerably more decisive and final.

> "If any man has a stubborn and rebellious son who will not obey his father or his mother, and when they chastise him, he will not even listen to them, then his father and mother shall seize him, and bring him out to the elders of his city at the gateway of

1. John White, *Parents in Pain* (Downers Grove, Ill.: InterVarsity Press, 1979), p. 201.

his home town. And they shall say to the elders of his city, 'This son of ours is stubborn and rebellious, he will not obey us, he is a glutton and a drunkard.' Then all the men of his city shall stone him to death; so you shall remove the evil from your midst, and all Israel shall hear of it and fear." (Deut. 21:18–21)

These measures appear brutal and extreme, but God viewed the sin of rebellion as seriously as He did the worship of demons and idols.

"For rebellion is as the sin of divination,
And insubordination is as iniquity and idolatry."
(1 Sam. 15:23a)[2]

An Illustration from the Old Testament

Though devoted to serving as a priest before God, Eli responded passively to the brash rebellion of his two sons (1 Sam. 2:23–25a). Because of his tolerance, shame was brought not only on his house but on the house of God (vv. 12–17, 22, 29–30). And because Eli didn't face the seriousness of the problem and stop his sons, God stepped in and did it for him.

"In that day I will carry out against Eli all that I have spoken concerning his house, from beginning to end. For I have told him that I am about to judge his house forever for the iniquity which he knew, because his sons brought a curse on themselves and he did not rebuke them." (3:12–13; see also 2:31–36)

The methods of dealing with a rebellious child change from the Old Testament to the New. As we look at the love expressed by the father of the prodigal son, we'll see that it's still an example of tough love, but it is gracious in its means and redemptive in its goal.

---

2. Opposition to God is the common denominator between rebellion and divination. Rebellion opposes God's authority directly. Divination opposes it indirectly by worshiping forces antagonistic to God. Insubordination is like idolatry in that "all conscious disobedience . . . makes self-will, the human I, into a god. . . . All manifest opposition to the word and commandment of God is, like idolatry, a rejection of the true God." C. F. Keil and F. Delitzsch, *Commentary on the Old Testament* (reprint, Grand Rapids, Mich.: William B. Eerdmans Publishing Co., 1982), vol. 2, p. 157.

Christ's Parable of a Rebellious Son

Acclaimed by literary critics as the greatest short story ever written, the parable of the Prodigal Son is a classic illustration of how to deal with rebellion in a Christlike way.

The Setting

The story is set in first-century Palestine, but the drama is contemporary, enacted every day across the world.

> And [Jesus] said, "A certain man had two sons; and the younger of them said to his father, 'Father, give me the share of the estate that falls to me.' And he divided his wealth between them. And not many days later, the younger son gathered everything together and went on a journey into a distant country." (Luke 15:11–13a)

Jewish law said that when a family had two sons, the elder would get two-thirds of his father's estate and the younger would get the remaining third at his father's retirement or death. Given the younger brother's rivalry with his more dutiful older brother, the prodigal son undoubtedly felt that when his father died the older brother would take the prime pastureland and he would get stuck with the rocky back-forty. Because of these tensions at home and because of a craving to see the world, the younger son decided to leave home.

Did you notice his father's response to this decision? "And he divided his wealth between them." No argument, no tears, no self-righteous refusal. Just the silent eloquence of his opened hand.

Deciding to let his son leave was probably the most heartrending choice this father ever faced. Yet his love for his son overcame any reluctance he had. Again we turn to John White:

> Parents who are reluctant to take drastic steps should ask themselves why. Are they too scared? There is every reason to be scared. What parent is not? The thought of exposing a child to physical hardship, to loneliness and to moral temptation flies in the face of every parental instinct. . . .
>
> Yet love must respect the dignity, the personhood of the beloved. You cannot love someone truly and deny that person the dignity of facing the results

of his or her decisions. To do anything else would be to betray true love for something less than love, a "love" tainted by selfishness and weakness. Paradoxically we cannot love unless we risk the doom of the one we love.[3]

And what a "doom" this prodigal boy was about to face.

The Lifestyle

Having slipped off the collar of domestic responsibility, the younger son trotted off to answer the call of the wild, "and there he squandered his estate with loose living" (v. 13b). The prodigal's eat-drink-and-be-merry lifestyle eventually slid him into a moral and financial pigsty.

> "Now when he had spent everything, a severe famine occurred in that country, and he began to be in need. And he went and attached himself to one of the citizens of that country, and he sent him into his fields to feed swine. And he was longing to fill his stomach with the pods that the swine were eating, and no one was giving anything to him." (vv. 14–16)

The Return

With his funds exhausted, the pleasure seeker became a pauper, caught in the ravenous jaws of a famine. But with the crunch at its worst, he came to his senses. He shook loose from his circumstances and, with his tail between his legs, slinked home.

> "When he came to his senses, he said, 'How many of my father's hired men have more than enough bread, but I am dying here with hunger! I will get up and go to my father, and will say to him, "Father, I have sinned against heaven, and in your sight; I am no longer worthy to be called your son; make me as one of your hired men."' And he got up and came to his father." (vv. 17–20a)

What turned this wayward son's heart toward home? A mental picture of his father . . . a picture that gains color and depth when we realize that the son never visualized his father turning him away.

3. White, *Parents in Pain*, pp. 204, 206.

114

The Response

Verses 20b–24 resemble a climactic scene in an Academy Award-winning film. As you read, feel the emotion, the ecstasy, the tears of joy.

> "But while he was still a long way off, his father saw him, and felt compassion for him, and ran and embraced him, and kissed him. And the son said to him, 'Father, I have sinned against heaven and in your sight; I am no longer worthy to be called your son.' But the father said to his slaves, 'Quickly bring out the best robe and put it on him, and put a ring on his hand and sandals on his feet; and bring the fattened calf, kill it, and let us eat and be merry; for this son of mine was dead, and has come to life again; he was lost, and has been found.' And they began to be merry."

Our Dealings with an Older Rebel

If you have a rebel at home who wants to break with the family, here are some important principles to consider.

First: *No rebellious child should be allowed to ruin a home.* No matter how gifted, no rebel should be saved at the sacrifice of the entire family. John White adds a helpful dimension to this dilemma.

> The decision to dismiss children from home should not be made either because it will work or as a matter of expediency. It should be made on the basis of justice. And justice must consider every side of the problem. Is it morally just to keep children at home when other family members suffer deprivation in one form or another because of them?[4]

Second: *Principle must prevail over the person.* Again, justice must rule, impartially and without respect to persons—even if that person is your child. If an eternal principle is at stake, as with Eli's sons, stand on the principle, even if that means standing against your own flesh and blood. Take a look at some further wisdom from John White.

---

4. White, *Parents in Pain*, pp. 204–5.

God respected the dignity of our primal forefathers. He could have prevented their tragic disobedience and could thus have circumvented all the tragedies of human existence. He gave them a choice. They chose rebellion. He was then obliged to drive them from the garden.

If God so respects the autonomy he gave us, then we also must do the same for our children. In their earliest years they are not ready to be given full control of their lives because they are too vulnerable, too weak, too inexperienced to use it. But when the time comes, and that time must be decided by the parents as they wait on God, we must give them the dignity of letting them face the real consequences of their actions.

To do so will be painful. If ever you find yourself in that position, beware of sealing your heart in bitterness. The test of godly maturity will be to carry out the sentence combining tenderness with firmness.[5]

Third: *When true repentance occurs, God honors a forgiving response and a loving welcome.* The parable of the Prodigal Son should really be titled the parable of the compassionate father. For it is not the repentance of the son that overwhelms us; it's the all-embracing love of the father. And as the parable implies, when we joyfully embrace repentant sinners, we are most like our Father in heaven. This mental picture not only brings sinners back to God, but rebellious children back to the waiting arms of their parents.

🍇 *Living Insights* STUDY ONE

Go back to the story of the Prodigal Son for a moment and put yourself in the father's position. How would it feel if this had been your son who rebelled?

You tried to reason with him but he wouldn't listen. He said he didn't want to hear or see you anymore. He doesn't care what you think. And nothing you say or do can stop him. He's gone. The son who used to follow you everywhere now seems bent on

---

5. White, *Parents in Pain*, pp. 206–7.

following the opposite of everything you taught him. And that hurts, deeply. How would you respond the moment you first saw this prodigal son a long way off?

Honestly now, if you were the father, would you run to this rebel before you even knew why he was returning? Perhaps he's coming to demand more money, not ask for forgiveness. Are you willing to risk being abused by him again and rush to him anyway? Don't forget, he was the one who rejected you and walked away. And now you're going to run to him? Why not wait? Or just turn away?

And will you embrace him? Can you simply forget all the hurtful words he hurled at you and cheerily dress him in your best robe? Are you anxious to shower this belligerent son with kisses? Admit it, aren't you the least bit suspicious of his sudden pious attitude? Is he really penitent? Or is he just sorry he got caught in a famine?

These are just a few of the hurtful feelings and thoughts that real parents of prodigal sons and daughters wrestle with. So what can we do to prepare our hearts to be as forgiving and gracious as the father in Jesus' story? In *When Your Kids Aren't Kids Anymore*, Jerry and Mary White offer three helpful suggestions.

- First, *stay in fellowship with God*. During traumatic times, we tend to focus exclusively on prayer and neglect feeding our spirits from the Word of God. Be sure to read consistently.[6] And if you're having trouble concentrating, then plan to read for short periods several times a day.

- Second, *protect your health*. Be aware that you are very susceptible to physical illness when you're stressed out. Intense emotional suffering will rob you of your sleep, your appetite, and your energy level. Learn to say no to optional activities and possibly even back away from some important commitments until the crisis is over. Pay more attention to your nutritional needs . . . give yourself a little extra sleep . . . and exercise.

- Third, *gather a support group of close friends* whose spiritual maturity has been proven, who are committed to prayer, and with whom you can share your hurts and hopes. This type of support and counsel is essential.[7]

6. A topical Bible may be especially useful, helping you find what the Scripture has to say about the specific issues you are dealing with.

7. Jerry and Mary White, *When Your Kids Aren't Kids Anymore* (Colorado Springs, Colo.: NavPress, 1989), pp. 166–68.

Can you think of some other suggestions for becoming forgiving and gracious? Use the space provided to write your own ideas, finding as many Scripture references for each as you can.

_____

_____

_____

_____

_____

_____

_____

_____

For further help, the Minirth-Meier Clinic has an audio cassette series called "Forgiveness: The Foundation of Recovery" which we highly recommend. To purchase these tapes, write to Minirth-Meier Clinic West, 260 Newport Center Drive, Suite 430, Newport Beach, CA 92660.

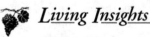 *Living Insights*

> We cannot love unless we risk the doom of the one we love.[8]

Are you considering risking the doom of a rebellious child? Before you decide to run that risk, let's examine the feelings inside you right now that are influencing this decision. Do you feel hurt? Angry? Depressed? Are you feeling guilty for not being a better parent? Put *all* of your feelings down without judging the rightness or wrongness of any of them.

_____

8. John White, *Parents in Pain*, p. 206.

_____

_____

_____

_____

_____

_____

_____

Everyone who has dealt with a prodigal son or daughter can identify with your feelings. They're intense, draining. And they make it very hard to think clearly and make wise decisions.

Perhaps if you wrote down your reasons for risking your child's doom it would help you cut through some of the emotions that are clouding your thinking.

Is an eternal principle at stake or simply differences of opinion or taste? If you feel it is an eternal principle, explain why and support your reasoning with Scripture.

_____

_____

_____

_____

_____

_____

Now, let someone outside the situation whose biblical wisdom you respect double-check your Scripture references and the way you're applying them to your situation.

If your reasoning is based simply on differences of opinion or taste, ask yourself, "Is this something worth risking my relationship with this child over?"

Chapter 14

FACING THE UNFORESEEN

Job 1:1–2:10; 42:5–6, 10–12

If we want to grow wise in family life, we have to give up some of our fantasies.

We like to view the family through the sentimental wire rims of Norman Rockwell: Father is at the head of the table, carving the Thanksgiving turkey; Mother is wearing her unsoiled apron, beaming over the meal in matronly elegance; children are gathered dutifully around the table—eager, wide-eyed, and rosy-cheeked. Truly a cornucopian Thanksgiving.

In real life, though, Dad is probably snoring on the couch to the tunes of halftime marching bands blaring from the TV. Mom is a limp dishrag after hours in the hot kitchen with a turkey that's too dry, dressing that's too soggy, gravy that's too lumpy, and rolls that are burnt on the bottom. And the kids? Well, the younger ones are pulling each other's hair out in the den; the pubescent son is locked in his room, his CD player throbbing to some alien pulse while he's chewing gum as if it were one of the four basic food groups. And the older daughter has been on the phone so long that, when she finally comes to the table, her head is fixed at a right angle.

Now that's real life. And taking a good look at it is the only way to get equipped for the unforeseen.

Life as It Is . . . Not as We Would Imagine

Cinderellas generally don't marry charming princes. Too few children can say with Dorothy, "There's no place like home." And in the real world, Father doesn't always know best. If we're going to see life as it really is, we must strip away our illusions. When you get down to basics, life consists of four key areas: people, events, decisions, and results.

People

Basically, by virtue of the Fall, people are sinful, selfish, and going through some kind of trouble.[1] We imagine, however, that they are good, giving, and living happily ever after.

Events

Many events that happen in our lives are unpredictable and surprising. We imagine, though, that to a large extent we can shape our destiny and predict what will happen.

Decisions

Many decisions we make are horizontal in scope and not necessarily aligned to biblical principles. We imagine, though, that our orientation is vertical. We believe that we received our marching orders from God when, in fact, we may have listened to society's drumbeat instead.

Results

The ramifications of our decisions are often far-reaching and painful to others. But we tend to imagine that we are autonomous beings and that our decisions affect only ourselves.

Life as It Was . . . Not as We Would Expect

Paging through the Scriptures, our thumb stops at the oldest book in the Bible—Job. Here we find the most ideal family we could possibly imagine.

An Enviable Family

Beginning with Job himself, we see that he was an ideal father.

> There was a man in the land of Uz, whose name
> was Job, and that man was blameless, upright, fear-
> ing God, and turning away from evil. (1:1)

So widespread was Job's renown that he was recognized as "the greatest of all the men of the east" (v. 3b). He had a wife and ten children (v. 2). He was affluent (v. 3). His children got along well (v. 4). And, most of all, Job took his relationship with the Lord

---

1. In contrasting the deeds of the flesh with the fruit of the Spirit, Paul shows which fruit grows naturally out of our old nature and which fruit sprouts naturally from our new nature (Gal. 5:19–23). In Ephesians 4:22–32 he again describes the two natures and shows that what springs out of the old self is a Pandora's box of sinful and self-serving deeds.

seriously (v. 5). It seems that Job's family life would have been a perfect picture for Norman Rockwell to capture on canvas. But as we will see, the colors on the palette turn suddenly dark and somber.

A Series of Calamities

Without a whisper of warning, Job's well-ordered life came crashing down around him like a house of cards. Within a span of minutes, four messengers reported to Job their devastating news.

> Now it happened on the day when his sons and his daughters were eating and drinking wine in their oldest brother's house, that a messenger came to Job and said, "The oxen were plowing and the donkeys feeding beside them, and the Sabeans attacked and took them. They also slew the servants with the edge of the sword, and I alone have escaped to tell you." While he was still speaking, another also came and said, "The fire of God fell from heaven and burned up the sheep and the servants and consumed them, and I alone have escaped to tell you." While he was still speaking, another also came and said, "The Chaldeans formed three bands and made a raid on the camels and took them and slew the servants with the edge of the sword; and I alone have escaped to tell you." While he was still speaking, another also came and said, "Your sons and your daughters were eating and drinking wine in their oldest brother's house, and behold, a great wind came from across the wilderness and struck the four corners of the house, and it fell on the young people and they died; and I alone have escaped to tell you." (vv. 13–19)

As we see Job's suffering, we easily share in his sorrow. What's not so easy is sharing his submissive response.

> Then Job arose and tore his robe and shaved his head, and he fell to the ground and worshiped. And he said,
> "Naked I came from my mother's womb,
> And naked I shall return there.

The Lord gave and the Lord has taken
   away.
Blessed be the name of the Lord."
Through all this Job did not sin nor did he blame
God. (vv. 20–22)

As if this bout hasn't been grueling enough, Satan gets another round with this battered believer and strikes a vicious body blow. From head to toe, Job is afflicted with boils (2:7–8). During this painful time, even his wife emotionally deserts him (vv. 9–10), leaving him to sift through the ashes of his spiritual confusion alone.

A Road to Recovery

For Job, the road to recovery will be long and winding through forty-two chapters of rugged introspection. Beginning in the first two chapters, he struggles to take four giant steps up that road.

First, there is the agony of humanity. There is shock, grief, pain, disbelief, and panic. The text says he "tore his robe and shaved his head" and "was sitting among the ashes" (1:20a, 2:8b). These were all outward manifestations of his inward grief.

Second, there is the struggle with theology. His wife, who could not make sense of the suffering, encourages him to "curse God and die" (v. 9). Surely Job wondered how God could permit such a thing and where He was during his hurt.

Third, there is an acceptance of reality. In 2:10 he responds to his wife: "'Shall we indeed accept good from God and not accept adversity?'"

Fourth, there is freedom from iniquity: "Through all this Job did not sin nor did he blame God" (1:22, 2:10b). While working through grief, the tendency is to blame others, even God. But Job suspends judgment and instead submits to suffering's yoke.

A Remarkable Restoration

With God's restorative touch, the gaping wound in Job's life is at last closed and finally healed.

> And the Lord restored the fortunes of Job when he prayed for his friends, and the Lord increased all that Job had twofold. Then all his brothers, and all his sisters, and all who had known him before, came to him, and they ate bread with him in his house; and they consoled him and comforted him for all the

evil that the Lord had brought on him.[2] And each one gave him one piece of money, and each a ring of gold. And the Lord blessed the latter days of Job more than his beginning, and he had 14,000 sheep, and 6,000 camels, and 1,000 yoke of oxen, and 1,000 female donkeys. And he had seven sons and three daughters. (42:10–13)

Life as It Will Be . . . Not as We Would Prefer

As the storms of life sweep over us, we bend and sway under their force. But shallow-rooted, slow-growing creatures that we are, we prefer sunshine to torrential rain and calm, idyllic days to wind-swept nights. We prefer no surprises. But in spite of our preferences, life remains untamed and unpredictable. We prefer protection from adversity—a shelter from the wind and rain. But life continues its pelting downpour. We prefer to watch the lightning and hear the thunder from a distance. But God brings the clouds near. Fortunately, though, He leads us through the storm . . . hand in hand . . . a step at a time (Ps. 23:4).

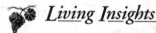 *Living Insights* STUDY ONE

It's true. If we want to grow wise in family life, we really do have to give up some of our fantasies.

And one fantasy that many of us refuse to let go of is that "good families are trouble-free families." But there's no such thing as a trouble-free family anymore than there's a Santa Claus. What *is* true, Dolores Curran discovered, is that in the past, good families

2. The word translated "evil" in Hebrew may also be translated as "misery, distress, injury." The word is used about twenty times to designate injury done to the body and about a dozen times to describe sorrow one may experience. Its use here denotes the sum of the distressing happenings of life. See the *Theological Wordbook of the Old Testament*, ed. R. Laird Harris, Gleason L. Archer, Jr., and Bruce K. Waltke (Chicago, Ill.: Moody Press, 1980), vol. 2, p. 856. This verse, which attributes Job's misery to God, poses an apparent contradiction with chapter 1, which attributes his suffering to Satan. Although God did not bring misery into Job's life Himself, by permitting Satan to do so, God can be looked at as ultimately sharing a degree of responsibility for what Job experienced. The difference between the responsibility of Satan and that of God was that Satan brought misery into Job's life with the intent of getting him to defect from God (1:9–11). God's intent, however, was to display Job as an example of integrity and patient endurance in the midst of trials (compare 2:3 with James 5:11).

were taught to hide their problems. And this in turn led to the fictionalized view that good families have no problems.[3]

Fortunately, this myth is slowly being replaced with the truth about families and problems—they're inseparable! "Good families" experience problems the same as the not-so-good. What makes the qualitative difference between families is *how* they handle them. Curran underscores this with a comparison.

> The "good" family of yesterday claimed it had no problems; today's healthy family expects a variety of problems. The "good" family of the past never admitted any need for help; today's healthy family is healthy because it is able to admit to need and seek help in the early stages of a problem. In fact, it might even be said that the healthier the family today, the sooner it is likely to admit its weakness and work on it publicly, a direct turnaround from a couple of generations ago when the best families were problemless.[4]

What about your family? Are you teaching your children to recognize and deal with problems effectively, biblically? Or are you raising them to believe in the destructive myth that a good marriage and family is a trouble-free marriage and family?

One way to find the answer to these questions is by examining how you deal with family problems.

Do you expect problems and view them as a normal part of life? If not, how would you describe your attitude toward them?[5]

_____

_____

_____

_____

Are potentially serious problems dealt with early on or only after a crisis develops? Can you give an example?

3. Dolores Curran, *Traits of a Healthy Family* (Minneapolis, Minn.: Winston Press, 1983), p. 258.

4. Curran, *Traits of a Healthy Family*, p. 258.

5. For help in developing a godly perspective, read and cross-reference James 1:2–4 and 2 Cor. 12:7–10.

How are family issues taken on? With a spirit of cooperation and confidence? Or do you refuse to face problems? Are secrecy and silence invoked as solutions?

How efficient is the family at coming to a decision? Does one person settle family problems quickly by ignoring the thoughts and feelings of the others? Or do you rely on negotiation—without manipulation or competitiveness—to arrive at a solution?

Are you equipping your family for the unforeseen by teaching them how to deal with their problems rather than deny them?

 Living Insights STUDY TWO

To talk about equipping for the unforeseen is nonsense! How can you equip for something you don't know is coming? None of us know when, where, or how calamity might strike anymore than Job did. So eat, drink, and be merry, for tomorrow a tornado may land in your living room. Right? Well, not exactly.

Though it is nonsense to talk of preparing for the unforeseen in any physical sense, preparing for the unforeseen *mentally* makes great sense. Job was prepared. Not for the enemies or the fire or the great wind, but for responding to the unforeseen with the right attitude (Job 1:20–22).

Like Job, we can't control our circumstances either, but we *can* choose how we will respond to them. Our attitude is something we *can* control. And whether or not we are prepared to respond in worship, as Job did, will determine how equipped we are to face the unforeseen.

Resentment, bitterness, hostility—these are the common attitudes people choose when they're mistreated. God, however, has a different choice in mind for His children. A choice we should demonstrate to our children as well.

> For what credit is there if, when you sin and are harshly treated, you endure it with patience? But if when you do what is right and suffer for it you patiently endure it, this finds favor with God. (1 Pet. 2:20)

How well-equipped to deal with the unforeseen are your children? Do they respond with patient endurance and worship like Job? Or are they willing to accept only good from God and not adversity? The answer can most likely be found by examining how *you* respond to daily unforeseen events like flat tires, sick children, and broken dishwashers. It's there in the crucible of ordinary living that our attitude toward the unforeseen is tested and refined. And our children's too.

Take a moment to evaluate what type of attitude toward the unforeseen is being developed in your children.

_____

_____

_____

_____

_____

Chapter 15

ENDURING THE
UNBEARABLE

2 Samuel 18:5–19:8

Pastors see a lot of pain. Chuck Swindoll, former pastor of the First Evangelical Free Church of Fullerton, California, once decided to keep a journal of the hardship he encountered in one thirty-six-hour period. Here's what he recorded:

- A mother and dad committed their teenager to a local psychiatric ward.

- A relative of a girl in our church took her own life.

- A fifteen-year marriage went up in smoke as the wife walked out. She is now living with another man.

- A young couple had their first child. She has Down's Syndrome.

- A young woman in her twenties is plagued with guilt and confusion because of an incestuous relationship with her father years ago.

- A young woman on a nearby Christian campus was raped and stabbed.

- A former minister is disillusioned. He has left the faith.

- A middle-aged husband and wife cannot communicate without screaming. Separation seems inevitable.

- An employer is embittered because his Christian employee cannot be trusted.

- A missionary wife who has returned to the States has suffered an emotional breakdown.

- Christian parents just discovered their son is a practicing homosexual.[1]

1. Charles R. Swindoll, *Three Steps Forward, Two Steps Back*, rev. ed. (Nashville, Tenn.: Thomas Nelson Publishers, 1990), pp. 9–10.

Sooner or later, we all encounter unbearable hardship. We wonder if the storm will ever subside, if the darkness will ever pass. Take heart. For this chapter will not only encourage us to prepare for the unbearable but will help us persevere through it.

The Unbearable Is Inescapable

No one eludes the unbearable. It is an inescapable thorn of a fallen world, as indicated by Job, whose name has become synonymous with suffering.

> "For man is born for trouble,
> As sparks fly upward." (5:7)

Again, in 14:1, Job underscores the inevitability of human suffering.

> "Man, who is born of woman,
> Is short-lived and full of turmoil."

When the crush of circumstances pressures us, we instinctively cry out to God for relief. David, no stranger to grief himself, records one such cry in Psalm 102:1–7.

> Hear my prayer, O Lord!
> And let my cry for help come to Thee.
> Do not hide Thy face from me in the day of my
> distress;
> Incline Thine ear to me;
> In the day when I call answer me quickly.
> For my days have been consumed in smoke,
> And my bones have been scorched like a hearth.
> My heart has been smitten like grass and has
> withered away,
> Indeed, I forget to eat my bread.
> Because of the loudness of my groaning
> My bones cling to my flesh.
> I resemble a pelican of the wilderness;
> I have become like an owl of the waste places.
> I lie awake,
> I have become like a lonely bird on a housetop.

Somber, anguished words from the depths of a hurting heart. For the unbearable paid an unwelcome visit to David's house, a visit David wasn't sure he was equipped to handle.

The Unbearable Seems Unendurable

The particular unbearable situation that we'll be watching David endure concerns his son Absalom—handsome, intelligent, and furiously rebellious.

Family Background

David sweated through much of Absalom's life, for this rebellious son brought heated turmoil to the palace (2 Sam. 13–18). Early on, Absalom became disillusioned by his father's passive response to his sister Tamar's rape. He later grew deceitful and finally disloyal to his father, leading a revolt against the throne. Absalom's actions left many people confused, a few resentful, and one enraged —Joab, David's military commander.

Absalom's Death

During Absalom's coup, David fled from the throne rather than kill his own flesh and blood. Although their armies would soon clash in a fateful forest of oaks, the king made every effort to spare his wayward son.

> And the king charged Joab and Abishai and Ittai, saying, "Deal gently for my sake with the young man Absalom." And all the people heard when the king charged all the commanders concerning Absalom. (18:5)

The battle between Absalom's men and David's raged in the forest of Ephraim. But Absalom's forces were no match for the angry swords of David's mighty men (vv. 6–7). Absalom fled through the forest in defeat, and as he did, his long, flowing hair became entangled in the branches of a large oak tree. Like a fly caught in a web, he could not extricate himself. And with the nimble promptness of a spider, Joab rushed to devour his prey.

> Then Joab . . . took three spears in his hand and thrust them through the heart of Absalom while he was yet alive in the midst of the oak. And ten young men who carried Joab's armor gathered around and struck Absalom and killed him. (vv. 14–15)

David's Grief

Having taken refuge at the city of Mahanaim, David was anxiously awaiting news of his son's welfare. *Is it well with Absalom? . . . Is it well with Absalom?* he begged of Joab's messengers as they arrived (vv. 29, 32). When the truth of Absalom's death finally came out, David's grief seemed unbearable.

> And the king was deeply moved[2] and went up to the chamber over the gate and wept. And thus he said as he walked, "O my son Absalom, my son, my son Absalom! Would I had died instead of you, O Absalom, my son, my son!"
>
> Then it was told Joab, "Behold, the king is weeping and mourns for Absalom." And the victory that day was turned to mourning for all the people, for the people heard it said that day, "The king is grieved for his son." So the people went by stealth into the city that day, as people who are humiliated steal away when they flee in battle. And the king covered his face and cried out with a loud voice, "O my son Absalom, O Absalom, my son, my son!" (18:33–19:4)

Not only did his son's death seem unendurable, but his grief and remorse seemed unending. Alexander Whyte goes to the heart of David's anguish, finding the intense pain tinged with the ache of remorse.

> The terrible cry that comes out of the chamber over the gate . . . is the love of a heart-broken father, no doubt. But the pang of the cry, the innermost agony of the cry, the poisoned point of the dagger in that cry is remorse. I have slain my son! I have murdered my son with my own hands! I neglected my son Absalom from a child! With my own lusts I laid his very worst temptation right in his way. . . . If he rebelled, who shall blame him? I, David, drove Absalom to rebellion. It was his father's hand that stabbed Absalom through the heart. O Absalom, my murdered son![3]

---

2. The Hebrew word is *ragaz*. "The primary meaning of this root is to quake or shake. . . . Most usages of *ragaz* express agitation growing out of some deeply rooted emotion" like trembling in fear or raging in anger. *Theological Wordbook of the Old Testament*, ed. R. Laird Harris, Gleason L. Archer, Jr., Bruce K. Waltke (Chicago, Ill.: Moody Press, 1980), vol. 2, pp. 830–31.

3. Alexander Whyte, *Bible Characters* (London, England: Oliphants, 1952), vol. 1, pp. 312–13.

The Unbearable Is Not Unending

Although some pain seems unrelenting, it truly isn't. Remember Solomon's words? "There is an appointed time for everything. . . . A time to weep, and a time to laugh; A time to mourn, and a time to dance" (Eccles. 3:1a, 4). It may feel as if unbearable circumstances have wintered in your heart, but remember that seasons do change. At this point in David's life, however, winter had just fallen with a withering frost at the news of Absalom's death.

Joab's Counsel

Joab, who had seen the whole tragic story of Absalom's life unfold shamefully before all Israel, confronted David about the inequity of his narrowly focused grief. In bold, blunt words, he told David to face the truth and realize how his actions were affecting those around him.

> Then Joab came into the house to the king and said, "Today you have covered with shame the faces of all your servants, who today have saved your life and the lives of your sons and daughters, the lives of your wives, and the lives of your concubines, by loving those who hate you, and by hating those who love you." (19:5–6a)

David undoubtedly felt tremendous guilt about his relationship with Absalom. As a result, his tears blurred the fact that Absalom had been bent on destroying him and any of his people that stood in the way. Enraged that David didn't see how his self-absorbed grief was demeaning the loyalty of his people, Joab lashed out.

> "For you have shown today that princes and servants are nothing to you; for I know this day that if Absalom were alive and all of us were dead today, then you would be pleased." (v. 6b)

Having spoken his mind, Joab then went on to give his friend a wise piece of advice—affirm the ones closest to you, David.

> "Now therefore arise, go out and speak kindly to your servants, for I swear by the Lord, if you do not go out, surely not a man will pass the night with you, and this will be worse for you than all the evil that has come upon you from your youth until now." (v. 7)

Unbearable circumstances threw David into a vertigo of introspection. But Joab grabbed him by the shoulders, stood him on the ground, and got David to take his eyes off himself and place them onto those who were in desperate need of his affirmation.

David's Response

His perspective restored, the king heeded Joab's advice.

> So the king arose and sat in the gate. When they told all the people, saying, "Behold, the king is sitting in the gate," then all the people came before the king. (v. 8a)

Does this mean David was through grieving for Absalom? No. Was it possible to just go back to work and forget about him? No.

But perhaps returning to rule the kingdom was a significant beginning step in the healing process for David. A beginning that would lead to the end of this father's unbearable pain for a lost son.

C. S. Lewis went through a long grieving process when he lost his wife to cancer. You can follow the winding road that his grief took in his book *A Grief Observed*.

In his pain, he asked searching questions about his faith.

> Meanwhile, where is God? . . . Go to Him when your need is desperate, when all other help is vain, and what do you find? A door slammed in your face, and a sound of bolting and double bolting on the inside. After that, silence.[4]

It's completely natural when we're shouldering unbearable circumstances to cry out to God for relief. And when relief isn't immediate, it's easy to come to the same conclusion Lewis did. As we look at Lewis' grief sometime later, we see that the pain was not unending.

> Turned to God, my mind no longer meets that locked door. . . . There was no sudden, striking, and emotional transition. Like the warming of a room or the coming of daylight. When you first notice them they have already been going on for some time.[5]

4. C. S. Lewis, *A Grief Observed* (New York, N.Y.: Bantam Books, 1961), p. 4.

5. Lewis, *A Grief Observed*, p. 71.

God has His way of healing our wounds, and just as certain as there will be a time to weep, there will also—though it may seem unbelievable now—be a time to laugh again.

The Unbearable Can Be Endured

In closing, we want to distill the bubbling turmoil of David's life into principles that can equip us to endure the unbearable. First, we need to be realistic. Tragedy will likely touch all of us at some time or another. But as long as we deny that reality, we won't be prepared to handle it when it does come.

Second, we need a friend who is honest. David's life was filled with such friends, tracing back to Jonathan and Nathan. We all need friends who can put an arm around us while telling us the truth . . . friends like the one described in Proverbs 27:5–6.

> Better is open rebuke
> Than love that is concealed.
> Faithful are the wounds of a friend,
> But deceitful are the kisses of an enemy.

And although Joab wasn't the perfect model of a friend, he was forthright with David . . . and faithful.

Third, we need a Savior who is reliable, who is the same yesterday, today, and forever (Heb. 13:8); who will never leave or forsake us no matter what happens (v. 5); and who will be with us always, taking our hand as we go up the hills or down through the valleys (Matt. 28:20b). We have such a Savior in the Lord Jesus, who's waiting for us to turn to Him in our unbearable situations.

Finally, we need a faith that is sure, a faith that realizes all of our experiences are not intrinsically good, but in God's redemptive grace they work together *for* good (Rom. 8:28).

Living Insights

STUDY ONE

Though his warriors had been victorious, David felt completely vanquished by the news of Absalom's death. He couldn't congratulate his soldiers, feel joy, give direction . . . nothing. For a time, the ruler was ruled by pain and just wanted to be left alone.

Everyone who has suffered an unbearable event can empathize with David. After a crushing blow, you need time to heal before you're thrust back out to meet the needs of others.

But David was more than just a father, he was king. Thousands of people desperately needed his affirmation and leadership in that crisis. And there's the rub. On the one hand, David's pain screamed at him to shut the world out, while on the other, Joab vehemently protested that he take care of his people.

As parents in unbearable situations, we face a similar rub. We struggle just to deal with our own pain, but then there are the children. Who will help them with their pain? How will they survive the unbearable? Surprisingly enough, many parents unwittingly leave them to sink or swim completely on their own.

Why? Because we parents often mistakenly think that children are too young to understand; that if we can just keep things from them, they won't be affected. For example, studies have shown that more than sixty percent of children ages two to five are *not* permitted to attend the funeral of a deceased parent. Similar studies have also found that few children are even given the opportunity to express their grief during such an unbearable family trial. But Dr. John Sargent, a child psychiatrist and pediatrician at the Children's Hospital in Philadelphia, points out that what really hurts a child is *not* knowing what is happening and feeling shut out.[6]

Children may not share our level of understanding about the death of a parent, for example, but they do suffer the pain of loss *the same as we do*. "Protecting them" by not allowing them to deal with their loss only puts barriers in the way of their healing.

Are you in the midst of something unbearable? Have you become so preoccupied with your own grief that you have forgotten your children are hurting too?

In *Through the Valley of Tears*, authors Cyril Barber and Sharalee Aspenleiter offer ten suggestions for helping children deal with the tragedy of losing a parent. Whatever your unbearable circumstance, take a moment to read through and adapt this wisdom to your needs. Then do as David learned from Joab's counsel: arise, go out, and speak kindly to your children.

1. Allow them to observe and participate in your fears and vulnerability as well as in your mourning.

---

6. Cyril J. Barber and Sharalee Aspenleiter, *Through the Valley of Tears* (Old Tappan, N.J.: Fleming H. Revell Co., 1987), pp. 51–52, 67, 79.

2. Be willing to bear the pain of their loss as they unburden themselves to you.

3. Show your deep concern for them and provide a secure, caring environment in which they can give reasonable expression to their feelings without fear of censure.

4. Encourage them to verbalize their sense of loss and give them support throughout the mourning process.

5. Openly discuss the facts of death with them and allow them to understand more of the reality of the Christian faith and hope.

6. Allow them to work through their feelings of ambivalence toward the parent they have lost, and at the same time assist them in working through relational problems with other siblings and with other children in school.

7. Be willing to reminisce with them over the good times as well as the bad, without causing them to feel criticized for any attitudes they may express.

8. Be available to answer questions, but allow them free time to grow through the experience themselves.

9. Observe any "magical thinking" that would fantasize death, and bring their views back to reality.

10. Reassure them of your commitment to them and of the fact that you are not likely soon to die, too.[7]

🍇 *Living Insights*   STUDY TWO

If you came to a bridge that didn't look sturdy, would you stop to examine your faith in the bridge, or would you examine the bridge itself? Common sense tells you to examine the bridge and, when you're satisfied that it's reliable, to cross over with confidence.

7. Barber, Aspenleiter, *Through the Valley of Tears*, pp. 59–60.

This simple truth is profoundly important when it comes to crossing over unbearable circumstances. Would you stop at a moment of crisis to examine your faith or the God upon whom that faith rests? Common sense, of course, would tell you to turn your eyes on the Lord. But there's not always a lot of common sense floating around when we're in the middle of a crisis. Many tend to get hung up on examining their faith, "Why is this happening? What is God trying to tell me? Is this a punishment for something I've done?" which often only alienates them from God.

The next time you face an unbearable circumstance and need someone who is sure and reliable to see you through, keep your eyes on the Lord, examine His character, and He will give you the confidence to cross over.[8]

Remember the bridge.

---

8. For further study, consider the following verses: Psalms 19:9; 23:1; 90:1–2; 116:5; Nahum 1:7; James 1:17; 1 Peter 1:15; 1 John 1:5; 4:8. You might also want to read Cyril Barber and Sharalee Aspenleiter's book *Through the Valley of Tears*, which has three chapters devoted to teaching parents how to help their children through the grieving process.

Chapter 16

ANTICIPATING THE UNUSUAL

Genesis 6–9; Hebrews 11:7

C harlie Steinmetz had one of the greatest minds in electronics that the world has ever known. In fact, he built the mammoth generators for Henry Ford's first automobile plant in Dearborn, Michigan. One day, one of those generators broke down, and the plant screeched to a halt. Unable to get the generator going again, Ford called Steinmetz.

He came and puttered around the plant for a few hours. Tinkering with a few gauges, Steinmetz turned this, adjusted that, and then threw a switch that put the massive plant back into operation. A few days later, Ford received a bill from Steinmetz for $10,000. Surprised, Ford returned the bill with this note: "Charlie, isn't this bill just a little high for a few hours of tinkering around on those motors?"

Steinmetz returned an itemized bill to Ford:

For Tinkering Around on the Motors: $ 10
For Knowing <u>Where</u> to Tinker: 9,990
Total: $10,000

Ford paid the bill with a smile. For what appeared to be of little value was, in fact, of greatest value—an entire assembly line depended on Steinmetz's knowledge.[1]

We've been tinkering with the subject of how to equip families for life. But behind the scenes, tapping gauges and turning switches, is the Holy Spirit. And He knows just where to tinker, doesn't He? We've puttered around with the subject of the unforeseen and the unbearable. Now we want to turn our attention to the unusual so we can be equipped to understand God's standard operating procedure.

---

1. From *Healing for Damaged Emotions*, by David A. Seamands (Wheaton, Ill.: Victor Books, 1981), p. 23.

In God's Family . . . An Unusual Operating Procedure

God's *modus operandi* is the great, the unsearchable, and the miraculous, as Eliphaz confirms in Job 5.

> "But as for me, I would seek God,
> And I would place my cause before God;
> Who does great and unsearchable things,
> Wonders without number." (vv. 8–9)

In verses 10–16, we see the incredible ways God works in people's lives.

> "He gives rain on the earth,
> And sends water on the fields,
> So that He sets on high those who are lowly,
> And those who mourn are lifted to safety.
> He frustrates the plotting of the shrewd,
> So that their hands cannot attain success.
> He captures the wise by their own shrewdness
> And the advice of the cunning is quickly thwarted.
> By day they meet with darkness,
> And grope at noon as in the night.
> But He saves from the sword of their mouth,
> And the poor from the hand of the mighty.
> So the helpless has hope,
> And unrighteousness must shut its mouth."

God's workings give hope to the lowly and defenseless, while dumbfounding the high and mighty. The New Testament counterpart to this passage is Romans 11:33.

> Oh, the depth of the riches both of the wisdom
> and knowledge of God! How unsearchable are His
> judgments and unfathomable His ways!

Stop for a minute and think through the Bible. It's just bursting at the seams with the incredible ways God works. The parting of the Red Sea. Manna from heaven. The pillars of cloud and fire to guide Israel in the wilderness. Jericho's wall. The Virgin Birth. Water into wine. Feeding the five thousand. Healing after healing. The Resurrection. And the list goes on and on. God still desires to do the unusual and the unsearchable . . . but are we open to that? Are we ready? Are we willing to let Him work in unusual ways?

In Noah's Family . . . A Study in Surprises

Noah's family was no different than ours—with one exception. They were open, ready, and willing to be a part of God's plan, even if that plan seemed highly unusual.

Difficult Times in Which to Live

Noah and his family grew up in an ungodly culture. Depravity paraded the streets in a raucous Mardi Gras of immorality.

> Then the Lord saw that the wickedness of man was great on the earth, and that every intent of the thoughts of his heart was only evil continually. And the Lord was sorry that He had made man on the earth, and He was grieved in His heart. . . .
> Now the earth was corrupt in the sight of God, and the earth was filled with violence. And God looked on the earth, and behold, it was corrupt; for all flesh had corrupted their way upon the earth. (Gen. 6:5–6, 11–12)

Lest we place too much emphasis on the environment's role in shaping character, note that in the midst of this cesspool society there arose an unsoiled saint.

> But Noah found favor in the eyes of the Lord.
> These are the records of the generations of Noah. Noah was a righteous man, blameless in his time; Noah walked with God. (vv. 8–9)

Righteous before God and blameless before others, Noah was like a salmon swimming upstream against the swift and sordid currents of his culture.

A Frightening Prophecy and a Creative Plan

In verses 7, 13, and 17, God unveiled a sobering glimpse of the brimming cauldron of His wrath.

> And the Lord said, "I will blot out man whom I have created from the face of the land, from man to animals to creeping things and to birds of the sky; for I am sorry that I have made them." . . .
> . . . Then God said to Noah, "The end of all flesh has come before Me; for the earth is filled with

violence because of them; and behold, I am about to destroy them with the earth. . . . And behold, I, even I am bringing the flood of water upon the earth, to destroy all flesh in which is the breath of life, from under heaven; everything that is on the earth shall perish."

But before His wrath spilled over to inundate the world, God arranged a creative plan of deliverance for righteous Noah.

"Make for yourself an ark of gopher wood; you shall make the ark with rooms, and shall cover it inside and out with pitch. And this is how you shall make it: the length of the ark three hundred cubits, its breadth fifty cubits, and its height thirty cubits." (vv. 14–15)

This ark would measure 450 feet long, 75 feet wide, and 45 feet high and have the same volume as 522 livestock railroad cars.[2] This request was highly unusual because *it had never rained before*, let alone flooded (2:5–6). But while a reprobate world scorned, God was in the process of saving a remnant—a small scrap of humanity who still believed in Him, still loved Him, still served Him (6:18–21).

Obedience, Deliverance, and a Blessing

Noah obeyed God and built the ark (v. 22), a task that took his family 120 years to complete (v. 3). At last the day came that would seal the fate of a decadent world.

Then the Lord said to Noah, "Enter the ark, you and all your household; for you alone I have seen to be righteous before Me in this time." (7:1)

Again Noah's obedience is underscored: "And Noah did according to all that the Lord had commanded" (v. 5). For forty days and forty nights the rains came (v. 12). Yet, in the midst of this destruction, God's deliverance was at work, saving everyone and everything in the ark (v. 23). When the water dried up, Noah built an altar to thank God for taking them safely through the storm (8:20–21). And He responded with His blessing.

---

2. These figures are based on a cubit of eighteen inches. Henry M. Morris, *The Genesis Record* (Grand Rapids, Mich.: Baker Book House, 1976), p. 181.

And God blessed Noah and his sons and said to them,
"Be fruitful and multiply, and fill the earth." (9:1)

Because of his incredible trust in God, Noah has been enshrined in the Hall of Faith of Hebrews 11.

By faith Noah, being warned by God about things not yet seen, in reverence prepared an ark for the salvation of his household, by which he condemned the world, and became an heir of the righteousness which is according to faith. (v. 7)

God asked Noah to believe and do some pretty incredible things; yet he trusted, and he obeyed.

By faith, Noah believed God's warning. By faith, he obeyed by building the ark. And by faith, he became an heir of righteousness. Is God asking you to believe and do some pretty incredible things right now? To trust Him when those around you are calling you a fool for doing so? Remember, they called Noah a fool too. And while he was on his way to Hebrews 11, they were left behind—treading water.

A Rainbow and a Reminder

To remind Noah of His covenant with the earth, God established a beautiful visual aid for all generations.

And God said, "This is the sign of the covenant which I am making between Me and you and every living creature that is with you, for all successive generations; I set My bow in the cloud, and it shall be for a sign of a covenant between Me and the earth. And it shall come about, when I bring a cloud over the earth, that the bow shall be seen in the cloud, and I will remember My covenant, which is between Me and you and every living creature of all flesh; and never again shall the water become a flood to destroy all flesh. When the bow is in the cloud, then I will look upon it, to remember the everlasting covenant between God and every living creature of all flesh that is on the earth." And God said to Noah, "This is the sign of the covenant which I have established between Me and all flesh that is on the earth." (Gen. 9:12–17)

Never again would God use rain to pour out His wrath upon the earth.

In Your Family . . . Some Practical Suggestions

Noah and his family model the importance of following God, even if the path of obedience is highly unusual, even if the road is steep, the way rocky, and the visibility poor. Here are a few suggestions that will better equip your family for the unusual.

First, remind your family that the unusual is God's standard operating procedure.

Second, keep in mind that He is still looking for families who will model His message. He is eager to write additional verses for Hebrews 11, and maybe one of those verses has your family's name on it.

Third, fight the tendency to prefer security over availability, to prefer today's comfort over tomorrow's challenge.

Finally, listen to your children when they urge you to do the unusual. Remember, God often speaks through them too. After all, the children were the ones who recognized Jesus as the Messiah and sang His praises, while the adults blindly criticized from afar (Matt. 21:15–16).

 Living Insights STUDY ONE

Emmanuel, Cardinal Suhard once wrote,

> "To be a witness does not consist in engaging in propaganda, nor even in stirring people up, but in being a living mystery. It means to live in such a way that one's life would not make sense if God did not exist."[3]

A living mystery. That was Noah all right, living his life in such a way that it could only make sense if God existed. How about your life? Are you a living mystery? Or have you played it safe, hedging your bets to make sure you won't look like a fool? Do people look at your life, as they did Noah's, and scratch their heads, wondering what in the world you're up to now? If not, maybe you're not

---

3. As quoted by Madeleine L'Engle in *Walking on Water: Reflections on Faith and Art* (Wheaton, Ill.: Harold Shaw Publishers, 1980), p. 31.

building a big enough boat. Maybe you're not trusting God for the unusual.

Write a list of a few unusual things God may be asking you to trust Him about.

_____

_____

_____

_____

_____

_____

Remind yourself that the unusual is God's standard operating procedure, and spend a few minutes praying about those things you wrote down. Pray that you would be available—available to do what God wants you to do or to go where He wants you to go. Who knows where that kind of faith might take you? Maybe to the hallowed halls of Hebrews 11!

🍇 *Living Insights*   STUDY TWO

In the twentieth century alone, many men and women have accomplished great works by faithfully following God's leading in the unusual. Some of these modern-day Noahs, however, made one grave mistake in building and launching their ministries—they forgot their families.

Noah made many sacrifices to build the ark, but the one thing he didn't sacrifice was his family. Under his supervision, they worked together to build the ark, and together they closed the doors behind them when the rains began.

Look back at the preceding Living Insight to the unusual things God may be asking you to trust Him about. Have you given much thought to how your family can be included in each of these? Take a moment to brainstorm some specific ways they can be involved.

_____

_____

_____

_____

_____

_____

_____

_____

Remember, it is never God's will to sacrifice your family in order to accomplish the unusual (compare Eph. 6:4; 1 Tim. 3:1–5; 5:8). Challenge them, show them how they can work by your side as you pursue your ark of the unusual.

Chapter 17

ACCEPTING THE UNDENIABLE

Isaiah 58:6–12; 2 Corinthians 13:7

If only.

Two words with slumped shoulders and downcast eyes that so often follow us through life. "If only I had known. . . . If only I could take back what I said. . . . If only I could undo what I did. . . ."

If only.

Words of regret. Words of shamed remembrance. Words that admit we've blown it.

The discouraging thing about studying Scripture is that we see how many mistakes we've made in life. Intellectual mistakes. Spiritual mistakes. Conversational mistakes. The list goes on and on. But no mistakes are as painful as people mistakes. Especially mistakes made with people we love—like our children.

Although it's impossible to turn back the clock, we *can* turn the negative memories of those mistakes into something positive.

Inescapable and Painful Realities of Humanity

"To err is human" is a shopworn sign we could all hang over our lives. No matter how much we regret them, mistakes are an inescapable part of our humanity. We are all imperfect—including our offspring. We cannot change the past—including the way we raised our children. And we are personally responsible for our own mistakes —including even innocent ones. A hastily woven blanket of rationalization can cover our mistakes with flimsy excuses, but it doesn't make them disappear. And an accusing finger pointed at others doesn't diffuse the blame; it only confuses it.

Guidelines for Recovery and Renewal

So how do we recover from the mistakes we've already made? For an alcoholic, the first step of recovery is to look people in the eye and say: "Hello. My name is so and so. I'm an alcoholic." This honesty and forthrightness is also needed by parents when they take that first step on the road to recovery after blowing it. Several guidelines will help you choose the right path to renewed relationships with your children.

Negatively: Things That Won't Help

Admitting your mistakes is an important step to overcoming them. But it won't help to think: "It's all my fault." Problems in relationships are seldom just one person's responsibility, even in parent-child relationships.

Parenting, at its best, is a complex and demanding task. At its worst, it's a no-win situation that can produce the most frustrating guilt trip in all of life. Although we are imperfect parents, we are not the antecedent to all our children's problems—even God, the only perfect parent, has trouble with His less-than-perfect children. John White underscores this in his excellent book *Parents in Pain*:

> Parents are admonished to bring up children properly. Children are admonished to respond wisely to parental correction. If both play their part all will be well. But it takes a parent-child team working in harmony to produce this happy result.[1]

Later in his book White comments:

> You cannot ever control another human being, even if that human being is your own child.[2]

Another thing to avoid is being too simplistic in our use of Scripture verses and biblical principles. God's Word is the light that guides our way, but it is not Aladdin's lamp. We can't rub it three times and—abracadabra!—expect a genie to appear and grant us our wishes. Proverbs 22:6 is a good case in point.

> Train up a child in the way he should go,
> Even when he is old he will not depart from it.

This verse usually holds true. But it is given to us as a principle, not as an absolute promise. As we all know, no matter how well taught they were in their youth, some children become prodigals.

1. John White, *Parents in Pain* (Downers Grove, Ill.: InterVarsity Press, 1979), p. 44.
2. White, *Parents in Pain*, p. 58.

A good way to keep from making absolutes out of general principles is to avoid shackling them to words like *never* and *always*. Another way is to distinguish biblical principles from promises. Promises are *invariably* so; principles are *usually* so.

Positively: Things That Will Help

In principle, there is a correlation in Isaiah 58 between how a nation can recover from mistakes and how a parent can. Although Isaiah wrote thousands of years ago to the Jewish nation, as we dust off his words we find they are as applicable today as they were the day they were written. The context of the passage finds Judah's relationship with God in ruins. God counsels the people not to go through the motions of fasting and repentance. Rather, He recommends true fasting.

> "Is this not the fast which I choose,
> To loosen the bonds of wickedness,
> To undo the bands of the yoke,
> And to let the oppressed go free,
> And break every yoke?" (v. 6)

God was looking for soft hearts that would care about what He cared about. This would provide the bedrock upon which He would rebuild their lives. From verses 7–12 we can fashion five important truths that will lay a sturdy foundation for the recovery and renewal of our relationship with our children.

First: *Humble yourself.* God wanted to see a humility of heart, one that would extend a caring hand to the hungry and the homeless.

> "Is it not to divide your bread with the hungry,
> And bring the homeless poor into the house;
> When you see the naked, to cover him;
> And not to hide yourself from your own flesh?
> Then your light will break out like the dawn,
> And your recovery will speedily spring forth;
> And your righteousness will go before you;
> The glory of the Lord will be your rear guard."
> (vv. 7–8)

The biggest obstacle to humility is pride. Pride keeps our necks stiff and our backs straight, a posture that has trouble bending before God and genuinely reaching out to others. By way of application to the family, if we lower ourselves in humility and admit our failure to our children, we will have taken a giant step toward recovery. As you relate to your children, is your attitude so fixed and rigid that you can't get down on their level?

Second: *Pray.* The result of a humble, repentant heart is obedient action. And the result of obedient action is heard prayer.

> "Then you will call, and the Lord will answer;
> You will cry, and He will say, 'Here I am.'" (v. 9a)

Our prayers are hindered when we are out of fellowship with God and each other (see 1 Pet. 3:7). And that's something we can't afford to have happen, because praying for our children is vital to any hope of rebuilding the broken walls in our relationships.

Third: *Remove the yoke.* The next bit of rubble the people had to clear away from their spiritual lives is found in the second half of verse 9.

> "Remove the yoke from your midst,
> The pointing of the finger, and speaking
> wickedness."

Do you want to break the constricting yoke that chafes your relationship with your children? Then ease the heavy load of blame from their shoulders—withdraw the pointing finger and stop hurling accusations. Change your attitude . . . and your heart.

Fourth: *Make yourself available and vulnerable.* Verses 10–11 tell us that God will bless us and meet our needs if we give ourselves for the needs of others.

> "And if you give yourself to the hungry,
> And satisfy the desire of the afflicted,
> Then your light will rise in darkness,
> And your gloom will become like midday.
> And the Lord will continually guide you,
> And satisfy your desire in scorched places,
> And give strength to your bones;
> And you will be like a watered garden,
> And like a spring of water whose waters do not fail."

Are you available to your children when they hunger for attention? Are you supportive when their esteem is afflicted? There is great encouragement here to all of us who've blown it. No matter how dark the shadows that stalk us from the past, God can outshine those haunting memories with the light of His grace. He can take a desert of conflict and transform it into a verdant valley of peace.

Fifth: *Trust God to bring the changes*. Though the people's relationship with God was in a ramshackle condition, it could still be rebuilt. It would have to be done from the ground up, but God would give His people the strength to do it.

> "And those from among you will rebuild the ancient
>   ruins;
> You will raise up the age-old foundations;
> And you will be called the repairer of the breach,
> The restorer of the streets in which to dwell." (v. 12)

The rubble of a ruined relationship with a child often takes no less work; sometimes it takes more because our children are not always as ready to forgive as God is. However, when your children see you investing your time in rebuilding the ruins, things have a good chance of changing, especially your children's perspective of you. They will begin to see you as a repairer and a restorer instead of a destroyer. In His time and in His way, God can rebuild relationships and restore foundations that were torn down years ago.

Essentials along the Way When Seeking to Rebuild

Restoring relationships, remember, doesn't often come quickly or easily. Solomon wrote of this truth in Proverbs 18:19,

> A brother [or child] offended is harder to be won
>   than a strong city,
> And contentions are like the bars of a castle.

Our mistakes have genuinely caused an offense, hurting our children deeply. And their resistance, their reluctance to respond to us, their defensiveness are like the strong bars of a well-guarded castle. In other words, they may not jump at the chance to forgive us right away. Which brings us to three essentials to keep in mind when we attempt the delicate work of rebuilding our relationships.

First, *have the right motive*. Be honest—don't manipulate your child. Second, *be patient*. It took time for your relationship with your child to get where it is today. It's only reasonable that the rebuilding process could take as long—and take much more work. Third, *do it all in God's strength*. Invariably, God's strength manifests itself in our weakness (2 Cor. 12:9–10; Phil. 4:13).

150

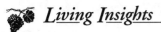 *Living Insights*

If there's one constant about parenting, it's making mistakes. But that doesn't mean we are all fated to be wretched parents. Some moms and dads obviously manage to do a great job of parenting despite their blunders. How do they do this? How do they preserve a good relationship with their children and teach them the right things in the midst of blowing it over and over again?

Perhaps the answer can be found in our own lives. Can you remember a time when one of your parents badly wronged you but later *humbly* asked for your forgiveness? Think about it for a moment. Relive that moment when he or she came to confess the wrong and ask for forgiveness. It had a profound impact on you, didn't it? All the sermons on humility combined probably couldn't match the power or impact of that one example. It affirmed that person's integrity, it restored and enhanced your respect for that parent, and it strengthened your ability to be compassionate and forgiving.

Admitting mistakes, especially to our children, is not easy. But when we do, we model such godly traits as humility, integrity, and a Christlike love, which have great power to restore relationships and mold character.

Of course, if your parents refused to admit their mistakes, then you learned powerful lessons in the deceitful arts of *denial*—"It wasn't my fault"; *blame*—"She did it first"; and *rationalization*—"He made me." Over time, the unresolved wrongs in relationships like this stack up into barriers, blocking almost every level of communication except the most superficial.

Mistakes will happen, but they won't ruin a family. How we handle them, however, can. Is there something right now that you have done wrong but haven't confessed and resolved with one of your children? Identify it.

_____

_____

If you're serious about seeking forgiveness and healing the wounds in that relationship, use the following questions from our study to help you prepare. Put a check by each one you are able to do.

Are you willing to:

❑ Put away your pride and humble yourself?

☐ Pray about it?

☐ Remove the yoke of blame?

☐ Make yourself available and vulnerable?

☐ Trust God to bring the changes?

🍇 *Living Insights*　　　　　　　　　　　　　　　　STUDY TWO

Isn't it true—we all want the other person to apologize first before we magnanimously offer to apologize ourselves. That is, of course, if we had planned to apologize at all. It may be that after we finish comparing our "harmless mistakes" with their "grossly unfair sins," we may smugly decide we shouldn't have to apologize about anything!

In our lesson today, however, we learned that the first step on the road to recovery is forthrightly and honestly admitting *our* mistakes—not our adversary's. Our focus isn't to be on comparing sins but rather on confessing them. Have we forgotten whom we serve? Are we not acting as though Christ doesn't even exist when we play these self-serving comparison games to decide whether to confess anything or not?

Have you blown it with one of your children lately? Are you willing to admit your mistakes and seek reconciliation, or are you waiting—too busy comparing? Use the space provided to write down what you think needs to be confessed and when you plan to do it.

What I need to confess: _____

_____

_____

_____

When I plan to do it: _____

Chapter 18

RELEASING THE REINS
Ephesians 4:11–16

O f all God's creatures, humans have the hardest time releasing their offspring. Bears have no trouble saying good-bye to their cubs. Wolves don't slump into depression once their litter is weaned and leaves home. And eagles literally push their eaglets out of the nest.

So why do humans instinctively want to hold on to their children? Why do we take so long to release the reins? Why do we try to keep our children in the nest when they should be out flying on their own?

Maybe we fear they're not quite ready for the real world. Maybe we feel we haven't done an adequate job of preparing them to face life. Unfortunately, keeping them in the nest offers no assurance that they will develop stronger wings. In fact, children who are coddled too long in the nest may never develop the strength to fly on their own. They grow into adults who lack self-confidence and the ability to think and act independently.

Releasing the reins allows children the opportunity to stretch their *own* wings. It is difficult to sit back and watch them leave, perched precariously on the edge of the nest, wings fluttering uncertainly. But that time of departure can be easier if we understand the process.

Progressive Cycles in Families

The first step in preparing to release your child is to understand the cycles that most families go through. Like the seasons, these stages overlap to a certain degree and vary in length, but basically they follow a definite progression.

Stage one: *Family founding.* This begins with the wedding and goes through the birth of the first child.

Stage two: *Childbearing.* This starts with the birth of the first child and lasts until the last child enters school.

Stage three: *Child rearing.* This lasts from the time the first child enters school until the last child enters college or leaves home.

Stage four: *Child launching.* Beginning with the first child's departure from home, this stage lasts until the last child leaves.

Stage five: *Empty nest.* All the children have left home now.

Each of these stages has its own struggles, but perhaps none is so heartrending as the fourth. Mothers who have wrapped their entire lives around their children sometimes become devastated when the children leave home. Fathers who have smothered their children with control sometimes become resentful when their authority is eclipsed by the children's independent steps toward freedom. But launching children from the nest needn't be a traumatic experience if certain principles are taken into consideration.

Preparation and Principles for Child Launching

In Ephesians 4, the primary application deals with the growth and development of our heavenly family—the church. However, we can also apply these principles to the growth and development of our earthly families. Verses 11–12 describe the role and responsibility of those special leaders in God's family.

> And He gave some as apostles, and some as prophets, and some as evangelists, and some as pastors and teachers, for the equipping of the saints for the work of service, to the building up of the body of Christ.

Just as God appointed leaders for the church, so He has designated parents to lead the family. Their job description? To equip and build up their children so that they might successfully survive the seasons of life. Here are some principles that will help prepare your children—and you—for that time of release.

Principle one: *Keep your role uppermost in mind.* Your role is equipping children for life—not keeping them near your side. You are to prepare them for adult life, as church leaders prepare their members.

> For the equipping of the saints for the work of service, to the building up of the body of Christ; until

we all attain to the unity of the faith, and of the
knowledge of the Son of God, to a mature man, to
the measure of the stature which belongs to the
fulness of Christ. (vv. 12–13)

Ultimately, church members must be loyal not to their leaders
but to the Lord. This is also true of the parent-child relationship.
Verse 12 describes the process of equipping, which leads to service,
which, in turn, leads to the overall health and growth of the body
of Christ. In this process parents, like church leaders, can know
they're on the right track when they see their children growing in
unity, increasing in the knowledge of God, becoming mature, and
incarnating the character of Christ.

Principle two: *Watch for signs of maturity and reward the result.*
Maturity unfolds at a different rate and fashion with each child.
Like the blooming of a flower, it shouldn't be forced. However, as
each petal of maturity unfurls itself, parents should recognize the
progress and reward it appropriately.

On the road to maturity, our children may also take an occasional detour or hit a chuckhole. When that happens, we, as parents, need to be there . . . to guide, to encourage, and to help
them find their way.

As a result, we are no longer to be children, tossed
here and there by waves, and carried about by every
wind of doctrine, by the trickery of men, by crafti-
ness in deceitful scheming; but speaking the truth
in love, we are to grow up in all aspects into Him,
who is the head, even Christ. (vv. 14–15)

Love doesn't stand at the side of the road in silence. Nor does
it shout, "I told you so!" Instead, love speaks the truth, in a con-
structive and gentle manner.

Principle three: *When an older child reverts to childishness, confront
the behavior with honesty and love.* The Bible doesn't take a sink-or-
swim approach to parenting. Parents aren't supposed to stand on
the riverbank passively watching their children wade into deep and
treacherous waters. Instead, we should follow Proverbs 27:5–6,
which gives some helpful advice for what to do when our children
make mistakes.

Better is open rebuke
Than love that is concealed.

Faithful are the wounds of a friend,
But deceitful are the kisses of an enemy.

Principle four: *Help your children discover and develop their own individuality, respecting it in a context of love.* Turning our attention again to Ephesians 4, we note that each and every member of Christ's body is unique and important.

> The whole body, being fitted and held together by that which every joint supplies, according to the proper working of each individual part, causes the growth of the body for the building up of itself in love. (v. 16)

When you treat your children as individuals, uniquely crafted by God for a special place in the body of Christ and in society, their sense of self-worth is enhanced. They then can see themselves as "fearfully and wonderfully made" instead of mass-manufactured on some celestial assembly line.

Two Rules to Remember

As we conclude this subject of releasing the reins, a couple of rules will help us let go.

Encourage Growth Rather Than Tolerate It

Growth is an evidence of life. Continued growth produces both maturity and stability, two qualities David prayed about for his children.

> Let our sons in their youth be as grown-up plants,
> And our daughters as corner pillars fashioned as for
> a palace. (Ps. 144:12)

Release Continually, Not Suddenly

Every year, release your grip a little bit more. In fact, you should begin releasing as soon as they are born. Remember, God has loaned your children to you for just a few years. They are borrowed treasure, not owned. You are trustees of that treasure, not titleholders. And when releasing your child seems an emotionally exhausting task, remember that God the Father set the example—releasing His only Son from the nest of heaven into our world.

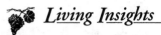

Most parents have little problem giving birth to their children, but many don't know whether to push, pull, or get out of the way when it comes to helping their teenagers develop their own identity. Perhaps it would help if we looked at it this way. During adolescence, the parents' role is more like that of a midwife. Our job is to assist our teens in their protracted struggle to emerge from the family womb as healthy, unique individuals.

Have the natural contractions of a teen wanting to become an adult begun in your home? The smoothness of the delivery in this interpersonal miracle depends a lot upon you, the parent.

To help you evaluate your midwifing capabilities, let's briefly examine three broad categories of parenting—healthy, midrange, and severely dysfunctional—and see how they encourage or hinder the development of a child's individuality.

◆

Healthy parenting, first of all, shows a deep respect for the unique experiences of each child. Children are allowed to see things differently from one another and still be accepted. Therefore, they express themselves more clearly and openly and take responsibility for their thoughts, feelings, and actions.

The more common parenting style is called *midrange*, which is characterized by a strict control of behavior and thought and a mistrust of feelings and drives. Control is the key word, allowing only limited growth of the individual's personal bents. Any thoughts or feelings that violate the family rules are simply not allowed. Thus, children learn to suppress and deny certain feelings and thoughts in order to be accepted by their parents.

In a *severely dysfunctional* parenting style, sameness is the overriding characteristic. These parents view individuality as rejection and therefore seek closeness in sameness. They show no respect for what their children think or feel by constantly telling them what they think and feel. For example, "Billy doesn't want to play now" or "You don't hate your sister; you love her just the same as she loves you." All boundaries of individual uniqueness and self-respect are blurred in favor of maintaining a swampy family sameness that is almost impossible to escape.

Of the three parenting styles, which characterizes yours best? Are you trying to make your children grow up to be just like you? Or are you allowing them to be all that God gifted them to be?

How are your children different from you? What differences are you encouraging? What are you not encouraging? Why? Are these moral issues or merely personal tastes?

_____

_____

_____

_____

_____

Are you allowing your children to see things differently and still be accepted? Can you give some specific examples?

_____

_____

_____

_____

_____

 Living Insights   STUDY TWO

Home is where life makes up its mind. And it makes up its mind largely based on the messages it receives there. The messages your children receive at home will be replayed throughout their formative years, shaping them into adults.

Those messages will reverberate in their memory to tell them what masculinity is . . . what femininity is . . . what a husband should be . . . what a wife should be . . . what a parent should be . . . what life should be. ·

The tape runs in a never-ending loop to echo every value you espouse—for better or for worse. What messages will you be sending to your children that you have learned from the last section of this study guide? In the space provided, write down specific truths and insights that have been meaningful for you.

III. Weathering the Storm

11. Warning the Uninvolved _____

_____

_____

_____

12. When Brothers and Sisters Battle _____

_____

_____

_____

13. Confronting the Unpleasant _____

_____

_____

_____

14. Facing the Unforeseen _____

_____

_____

_____

15. Enduring the Unbearable _____

_____

_____

_____

16. Anticipating the Unusual _____

_____

_____

_____

17. Accepting the Undeniable _____

_____

_____

_____

18. Releasing the Reins _____

_____

_____

_____

BOOKS FOR
PROBING FURTHER

I n the Old Testament, the word *wisdom* describes the technical skill needed in making priestly garments (Exod. 28:3), in crafting metalwork (31:3), and in executing the strategy of battle (Isa. 10:13).

In a more general sense, the word refers to the practical skill of living. The source of this skill is the all-knowing, all-powerful God of heaven. By His wisdom God numbered the clouds (Job 38:37) and established the earth (Prov. 3:19). He alone knows wisdom in its truest and most ultimate sense (Job 28:20, 23).

Proverbs tells us that the fear of the Lord is the beginning of wisdom (9:10). For only He can impart the wisdom that enables us to successfully navigate life's choppy and uncertain waters.

To help you navigate your way around the reefs that crop up from time to time, we have included a list of books for you to put on your ship's manifest. May God's Word steer your course and His Spirit fill your sails as you continue to grow strong and wise in family life.

Curran, Dolores. *Traits of a Healthy Family*. Minneapolis, Minn.: Winston Press, 1983. Curran discovered, through a survey conducted with five hundred family professionals, the top fifteen traits commonly found in the healthy family. She presents these traits with humor and sensitivity and provides guidance for incorporating them into our families.

Dobson, James. *The New Dare to Discipline*. Wheaton, Ill.: Tyndale House Publishers, 1992. Everyone with children will appreciate the balance between love and control that Dobson offers here. Built on a solid biblical premise, the book is buttressed by Dobson's strong background in psychology and is replete with examples from his own case studies. This is a completely revised edition of his 1970 classic in the field of child discipline.

———. *Hide or Seek*. Revised edition. Old Tappan, N.J.: Fleming H. Revell Co., 1979. In this excellent book, Dobson exposes the false set of scales with which our society weighs individual worth. He then shows the parent and teacher how to develop a strategy for cultivating self-esteem in children. This book will do more than help you understand your child; it will help you understand the forces that shaped you into the person you are today.

Ezzo, Gary and Anne Marie. Growing Families International. This organization provides excellent materials and courses for raising morally responsible children. "Growing Kids God's Way" and other classes are taught in local churches throughout the country. You can obtain information about classes and materials at 1-800-396-4GFI or visit their web site at http//:www.gfi.org.

The Focus on the Family Guide to Growing A Healthy Home. Mike Yorkey, general editor. Brentwood, Tenn.: Wolgemuth and Hyatt, 1990. This book is one of the single best resources on the family; it is an anthology or encyclopedia of articles on all aspects of family life.

Huggins, Kevin. *Parenting Adolescents.* Colorado Springs, Colo.: NavPress, 1989. Rather than offering formulas or "six easy steps" for producing perfect children, Huggins offers an honest look at the real issues that confront families with adolescents. His book is sound in its biblical foundation and challenging in its effect.

Hull, Karen. *The Mommy Book.* Grand Rapids, Mich.: Zondervan Publishing House, 1986. A practical and helpful guide for inexperienced mothers confronted by the often overwhelming demands of an infant.

Kimmel, Tim. *Little House on the Freeway.* Portland, Oreg.: Multnomah Press, 1987. In this warm and humorous book, the author pinpoints the marks of a hurried home fast on its way to self-destruction. With practical solutions, he shows how to restore calm and rest to your family.

Neff, LaVonne. *One of a Kind.* Portland, Oreg.: Multnomah Press, 1988. This book will show you how understanding personality types can help you better know and appreciate yourself and your loved ones. It will also explain how your children are unique and, therefore, why your parenting style should be tailored to each one.

Peterson, Eugene H. *Like Dew Your Youth: Growing Up with Your Teenager.* Rev. ed. Grand Rapids, Mich.: William B. Eerdmans Publishing Co., 1994. Peterson is one of the most insightful writers of our day. In this book he explains how to promote an atmosphere of communication, growth, honesty, forgiveness, and love between parents and adolescents. The study questions included at the end of each chapter make the book particularly useful for group discussion.

Schaeffer, Edith. *What Is a Family?* Old Tappan, N.J.: Fleming H. Revell Co., 1975. In appraising your family scene, probably no book will be as helpful as this one. A compelling mosaic of all that God intended the family to be.

Smalley, Gary. *The Key to Your Child's Heart.* Waco, Tex.: Word Books, 1984. This book centers around the principle of keeping your child's spirit open. Sharing frankly from his own family's experience, Smalley recounts what has and has not worked in his home and includes ways to draw your own family closer together.

Smalley, Gary, and John Trent. *The Blessing.* Nashville, Tenn.: Thomas Nelson Publishers, 1986. Our emotional and psychological makeup cries out for what the Bible calls "the blessing"— the knowledge that a parental figure loves and accepts us unconditionally. The authors detail the five elements of the blessing, how to bless others, and how to recover in cases where the blessing was withheld.

————. *The Language of Love.* Pomona, Calif.: Focus on the Family Publishing, 1988. This excellent book explores "emotional word pictures": a time-tested method of bridging the communication gaps that may exist between you and the people you love.

Swindoll, Charles R. *You and Your Child.* Nashville, Tenn.: Thomas Nelson Publishers, 1990. This book, besides providing much practical wisdom for family life, also contains helpful sections that deal with children who have special needs—including the adopted child, the handicapped child, and the single-parent child.

White, John. *Parents in Pain.* Downers Grove, Ill.: InterVarsity Press, 1979. A Christian psychiatrist, White offers his readers real comfort rather than pleasing panaceas or trifling tidbits that fail to help in times of crisis. His is a realistic book interspersed with illustrations that offer hope to parents in pain.

Some of these books may be out of print and available only through a library. For those currently available, please contact your local Christian bookstore. Books by Charles R. Swindoll may be obtained through Insight for Living. IFL also offers some books by other authors—please note the ordering information that follows and contact the office that serves you.

NOTES

NOTES

NOTES

NOTES

ORDERING INFORMATION

THE STRONG FAMILY
Cassette Tapes and Study Guide

This Bible study guide was designed to be used independently or in conjunction with the broadcast of Chuck Swindoll's taped messages which are listed below. If you would like to order cassette tapes or further copies of this study guide, please see the information given below and the order form provided at the end of this guide.

		U.S.	Canada
SFM	Study guide	$ 4.95	$ 6.50
SFMCS	Cassette series, includes all individual tapes, album cover, and one complimentary study guide	59.50	69.50
SFM 1–9	Individual cassettes, includes messages A and B	6.00	7.48

Prices are subject to change without notice.

SFM 1-A: *An Endangered Species?*—Deuteronomy 6:1–24
   B: *Masculine Model of Leadership*—1 Thessalonians 2:8–12

SFM 2-A: *Positive Partner of Support*—2 Timothy 1:1–7; Proverbs 24:3–4
   B: *Your Baby Has the Bents (Part One)*—Proverbs 22:6

SFM 3-A: *Your Baby Has the Bents (Part Two)*—Psalm 139:1–3, 13–16; 51:5
   B: *A Chip off the Old Bent*—Exodus 34:5–7

SFM 4-A: *Shaping the Will with Wisdom*—Selected Proverbs
   B: *Enhancing Esteem*—Ephesians 5:25–29; Selected Proverbs

SFM 5-A: *Challenging Years of Adolescence (Part One)*—Judges 11:1–8; 2 Samuel 13–16
   B: *Challending Years of Adolescence (Part Two)*—2 Chronicles 34:1–27; Daniel 1:3–21

SFM 6-A: *Warning the Uninvolved*—1 Samuel 1–4
   B: *When Brothers and Sisters Battle*—Selected Scriptures

SFM 7-A: *Confronting the Unpleasant*—Luke 15:11–24
B: *Facing the Unforeseen*—Job 1:1–2:10; 42:5–6, 10–12

SFM 8-A: *Enduring the Unbearable*—2 Samuel 18:5–19:8
B: *Anticipating the Unusual*—Genesis 6–9; Hebrews 11:7

SFM 9-A: *Accepting the Undeniable*—Isaiah 58:6–12;
2 Corinthians 13:7
B: *Releasing the Reins*—Ephesians 4:11–16

HOW TO ORDER BY PHONE OR FAX
(Credit card orders only)

Web site: http://www.insight.org

United States: 1-800-772-8888 or FAX (714) 575-5684, 24 hours a day,
7 days a week

Canada: 1-800-663-7639 or FAX (604) 532-7173, 24 hours a day, 7 days
a week

Australia and the South Pacific: (03) 9872-4606 from 8:00 A.M. to
5:00 P.M., Monday through Friday.
FAX (03) 9874-8890 anytime, day or night

Other International Locations: call the International Ordering Services
Department in the United States at (714) 575-5000 from 8:00 A.M.
to 4:30 P.M., Pacific time, Monday through Friday
FAX (714) 575-5683 anytime, day or night

HOW TO ORDER BY MAIL

United States
• Mail to: Mail Center
Insight for Living
Post Office Box 69000
Anaheim, CA 92817-0900
• Sales tax: California residents add 7.75%.
• Shipping and handling charges must be added to each order. See chart
on order form for amount.
• Payment: personal checks, money orders, credit cards (Visa, MasterCard,
Discover Card, and American Express). No invoices or COD orders available.
• $10 fee for *any* returned check.

Canada
- Mail to: Insight for Living Ministries
    Post Office Box 2510
    Vancouver, BC V6B 3W7
- Sales tax: please add 7% GST. British Columbia residents also add 7% sales tax (on tapes or cassette series).
- Shipping charges must be added to each order. See chart on order form for amount.
- Payment: personal cheques, money orders, credit cards (Visa, Master-Card). No invoices or COD orders available.
- Delivery: approximately four weeks.

Australia and the South Pacific
- Mail to: Insight for Living, Inc.
    GPO Box 2823 EE
    Melbourne, Victoria 3001, Australia
- Shipping: add 25% to the total order.
- Delivery: approximately four to six weeks.
- Payment: personal checks payable in Australian funds, international money orders, or credit cards (Visa, MasterCard, and Bankcard).

United Kingdom and Europe
- Mail to: Insight for Living
    c/o Trans World Radio
    Post Office Box 1020
    Bristol BS99 1XS
    England, United Kingdom
- Shipping: add 25% to the total order.
- Delivery: approximately four to six weeks.
- Payment: cheques payable in sterling pounds or credit cards (Visa, MasterCard, and American Express).

Other International Locations
- Mail to: International Processing Services Department
    Insight for Living
    Post Office Box 69000
    Anaheim, CA 92817-0900
- Shipping and delivery time: please see chart that follows.
- Payment: personal checks payable in U.S. funds, international money orders, or credit cards (Visa, MasterCard, and American Express).

Type of Shipping	Postage Cost	Delivery
Surface	10% of total order*	6 to 10 weeks
Airmail	25% of total order*	under 6 weeks

*Use U.S. price as a base.

Our Guarantee: Your complete satisfaction is our top priority here at Insight for Living. If you're not completely satisfied with anything you order, please return it for full credit, a refund, or a replacement, as *you* prefer.

Insight for Living Catalog: The Insight for Living catalog features study guides, tapes, and books by a variety of Christian authors. To obtain a free copy, call us at the numbers listed above.

Order Form
United States, Australia, and Other International Locations
(Canadian residents please use order form on reverse side.)

SFMCS represents the entire *The Strong Family* series in a special album cover, while SFM 1–9 are the individual tapes included in the series. SFM represents this study guide, should you desire to order additional copies.

Product Code	Product Description	Qty.	Price	Total
SFM	Study Guide		$ 4.95	$
SFMCS	Casette Series with study guide		59.50	
SFM-	Individual cassette		6.00	
SFM-	Individual cassette		6.00	
SFM-	Individual cassette		6.00	

Order Total

Amount of Order	First Class	UPS
$ 7.50 and under	1.00	4.00
$ 7.51 to 12.50	1.50	4.25
$12.51 to 25.00	3.50	4.50
$25.01 to 35.00	4.50	4.75
$35.01 to 60.00	5.50	5.25
$60.00 to 99.99	6.50	5.75
$100.00 and over	**No Charge**	

Rush shipping and Fourth Class are also available. Please call for details.

California Residents—Sales Tax
Add 7.75% of total.

UPS ❑   First Class ❑
Shipping must be added.
See chart for charges.

Non-United States Residents
Australia and Europe: add 25%.
Other: Price +10% surface or 25% airmail.

Gift to Insight for Living
Tax-deductible in the United States.

Total Amount Due $
Please do not send cash.

Prices are subject to change without notice.

Payment by: ❑ Check or money order payable to Insight for Living or
❑ Visa   ❑ MasterCard   ❑ Discover Card   ❑ American Express   ❑ Bankcard (In Australia)

Number

Expiration Date ___ / ___   Signature
We cannot process your credit card purchase without your signature

Name:

Address:

City: State:

Zip Code: Country:

Telephone: (   )   –   Radio Station:

If questions arise concerning your order, we may need to contact you.

Mail this order form to the Mail Center at one of these addresses:

Insight for Living
Post Office Box 69000, Anaheim, CA 92817-0900

Insight for Living, Inc.
GPO Box 2823 EE, Melbourne, VIC 3001, Australia

Order Form
Canadian Residents

(Residents of the United States, Australia, and other international locations,
please use order form on reverse side.)

SFMCS represents the entire *The Strong Family* series in a special album cover, while SFM 1–9 are the individual tapes included in the series. SFM represents this study guide, should you desire to order additional copies.

Product Code	Product Description	Qty.	Price	Total
SFM	Study Guide		$ 6.50	$.
SFMCS	Casette Series with study guide		69.50	.
SFM-	Individual cassette		7.48	.
SFM-	Individual cassette		7.48	.
SFM-	Individual cassette		7.48	.

	Subtotal .
	Add 7% GST .
	British Columbia Residents .
	Add 7% sales tax on individual tapes or cassette series.
	Shipping .
	Shipping and Handling must be added. See chart for charges.
	Gift to Insight for Living Ministries .
	Tax-deductible in Canada.
	Total Amount Due $.
	Please do not send cash.

Amount of Order	Canada Post
Orders to $10.00	2.00
$10.01 to 30.00	3.50
$30.01 to 50.00	5.00
$50.01 to 99.99	7.00
$100 and over	**No charge**

Loomis Courier is also available.
Please call for details.

Prices are subject to change without notice.

Payment by: ❏ Cheque or money order payable to Insight for Living Ministries or
❏ Visa ❏ MasterCard

Number

Expiration Date / Signature

We cannot process your credit card purchase without your signature.

Name:

Address:

City: Province:

Postal Code: Country:

Telephone: ( ) – Radio Station:

If questions arise concerning your order, we may need to contact you.

Mail this order form to the Processing Services Department at the following address:

Insight for Living Ministries
Post Office Box 2510
Vancouver, BC, Canada V6B 3W7

Order Form
United States, Australia, and Other International Locations
(Canadian residents please use order form on reverse side.)

SFMCS represents the entire *The Strong Family* series in a special album cover, while SFM 1–9 are the individual tapes included in the series. SFM represents this study guide, should you desire to order additional copies.

Product Code	Product Description	Qty.	Price	Total
SFM	Study Guide		$ 4.95	$.
SFMCS	Casette Series with study guide		59.50	.
SFM-	Individual cassette		6.00	.
SFM-	Individual cassette		6.00	.
SFM-	Individual cassette		6.00	.

Order Total .

Amount of Order	First Class	UPS
$ 7.50 and under	1.00	4.00
$ 7.51 to 12.50	1.50	4.25
$12.51 to 25.00	3.50	4.50
$25.01 to 35.00	4.50	4.75
$35.01 to 60.00	5.50	5.25
$60.00 to 99.99	6.50	5.75
$100.00 and over	**No Charge**	

California Residents—Sales Tax
Add 7.75% of total. .

UPS ❏ First Class ❏
Shipping must be added.
See chart for charges. .

Non-United States Residents
Australia and Europe: add 25%.
Other: Price +10% surface or 25% airmail. .

Gift to Insight for Living
Tax-deductible in the United States. .

Rush shipping and Fourth Class are also available. Please call for details.

Total Amount Due $.
Please do not send cash.

Prices are subject to change without notice.

Payment by: ❏ Check or money order payable to Insight for Living or
❏ Visa ❏ MasterCard ❏ Discover Card ❏ American Express ❏ Bankcard
(In Australia)

Number

Expiration Date / Signature

We cannot process your credit card purchase without your signature

Name:

Address:

City: State:

Zip Code: Country:

Telephone: ( ) – Radio Station:

If questions arise concerning your order, we may need to contact you.

Mail this order form to the Mail Center at one of these addresses:

Insight for Living
Post Office Box 69000, Anaheim, CA 92817-0900

Insight for Living, Inc.
GPO Box 2823 EE, Melbourne, VIC 3001, Australia

Order Form
Canadian Residents

(Residents of the United States, Australia, and other international locations, please use order form on reverse side.)

SFMCS represents the entire *The Strong Family* series in a special album cover, while SFM 1–9 are the individual tapes included in the series. SFM represents this study guide, should you desire to order additional copies.

Product Code	Product Description	Qty.	Price	Total
SFM	Study Guide		$ 6.50	$.
SFMCS	Casette Series with study guide		69.50	.
SFM- ☐	Individual cassette		7.48	.
SFM- ☐	Individual cassette		7.48	.
SFM- ☐	Individual cassette		7.48	.

	Subtotal	.
	Add 7% GST	.
	British Columbia Residents Add 7% sales tax on individual tapes or cassette series.	.
	Shipping Shipping and Handling must be added. See chart for charges.	.
	Gift to Insight for Living Ministries Tax-deductible in Canada.	.
	Total Amount Due $ Please do not send cash.	.

Amount of Order	Canada Post
Orders to $10.00	2.00
$10.01 to 30.00	3.50
$30.01 to 50.00	5.00
$50.01 to 99.99	7.00
$100 and over	**No charge**

Loomis Courier is also available. Please call for details.

Prices are subject to change without notice.

Payment by: ☐ Cheque or money order payable to Insight for Living Ministries or
☐ Visa ☐ MasterCard

Number | | | | | | | | | | | | | | | | | | |

Expiration Date | | | / | | | Signature | |

We cannot process your credit card purchase without your signature.

Name: | | | | | | | | | | | | | | | | | | | | | | | | | |

Address: | | | | | | | | | | | | | | | | | | | | | | | | | |

City: | | | | | | | | | | | | | | | | | | | Province: | | |

Postal Code: | | | | | | | Country: | | | | | | | | |

Telephone: (| | |) | | | – | | | | Radio Station: | | | |

If questions arise concerning your order, we may need to contact you.

Mail this order form to the Processing Services Department at the following address:

Insight for Living Ministries
Post Office Box 2510
Vancouver, BC, Canada V6B 3W7

Order Form
United States, Australia, and Other International Locations
(Canadian residents please use order form on reverse side.)

SFMCS represents the entire *The Strong Family* series in a special album cover, while SFM 1–9 are the individual tapes included in the series. SFM represents this study guide, should you desire to order additional copies.

Product Code	Product Description	Qty.	Price	Total
SFM	Study Guide		$ 4.95	$
SFMCS	Casette Series with study guide		59.50	
SFM- ☐	Individual cassette		6.00	
SFM- ☐	Individual cassette		6.00	
SFM- ☐	Individual cassette		6.00	

Order Total

Amount of Order	First Class	UPS
$ 7.50 and under	1.00	4.00
$ 7.51 to 12.50	1.50	4.25
$12.51 to 25.00	3.50	4.50
$25.01 to 35.00	4.50	4.75
$35.01 to 60.00	5.50	5.25
$60.00 to 99.99	6.50	5.75
$100.00 and over	**No Charge**	

Rush shipping and Fourth Class are also available. Please call for details.

California Residents—Sales Tax
Add 7.75% of total.

UPS ☐   First Class ☐
Shipping must be added.
See chart for charges.

Non-United States Residents
Australia and Europe: add 25%.
Other: Price +10% surface or 25% airmail.
Gift to Insight for Living
Tax-deductible in the United States.

Total Amount Due $
Please do not send cash.

Prices are subject to change without notice.

Payment by: ☐ Check or money order payable to Insight for Living or
☐ Visa   ☐ MasterCard   ☐ Discover Card   ☐ American Express   ☐ Bankcard
(In Australia)

Number

Expiration Date ☐☐ / ☐☐   Signature

We cannot process your credit card purchase without your signature

Name:

Address:

City: State:

Zip Code: Country:

Telephone: (   )   –   Radio Station:

If questions arise concerning your order, we may need to contact you.

Mail this order form to the Mail Center at one of these addresses:

Insight for Living
Post Office Box 69000, Anaheim, CA 92817-0900

Insight for Living, Inc.
GPO Box 2823 EE, Melbourne, VIC 3001, Australia

Order Form
Canadian Residents

(Residents of the United States, Australia, and other international locations,
please use order form on reverse side.)

SFMCS represents the entire *The Strong Family* series in a special album cover, while SFM 1–9 are the individual tapes included in the series. SFM represents this study guide, should you desire to order additional copies.

Product Code	Product Description	Qty.	Price	Total
SFM	Study Guide		$ 6.50	$.
SFMCS	Casette Series with study guide		69.50	.
SFM- ☐	Individual cassette		7.48	.
SFM- ☐	Individual cassette		7.48	.
SFM- ☐	Individual cassette		7.48	.

Subtotal .

Add 7% GST .

British Columbia Residents
Add 7% sales tax on
individual tapes or cassette series. .

Amount of Order	Canada Post
Orders to $10.00	2.00
$10.01 to 30.00	3.50
$30.01 to 50.00	5.00
$50.01 to 99.99	7.00
$100 and over	No charge

Loomis Courier is also available.
Please call for details.

Shipping
*Shipping and Handling must be added.
See chart for charges.* .

Gift to Insight for Living Ministries
Tax-deductible in Canada. .

Total Amount Due $.
Please do not send cash.

Prices are subject to change without notice.

Payment by: ☐ Cheque or money order payable to Insight for Living Ministries or
☐ Visa ☐ MasterCard

Number | | | . | | | | | | | | | | | | | | |

Expiration Date | | | / | | | Signature | |

We cannot process your credit card purchase without your signature.

Name: | |

Address: | |

City: | | Province: | |

Postal Code: | | Country: | |

Telephone: (| | | |) | | | | – | | | | | Radio Station: | | | |

If questions arise concerning your order, we may need to contact you.

Mail this order form to the Processing Services Department at the following address:

Insight for Living Ministries
Post Office Box 2510
Vancouver, BC, Canada V6B 3W7